Brownies

Sharon Moore

A FIRESIDE BOOK

Published by Simon & Schuster

New York   London   Toronto   Sydney   Tokyo   Singapore

Fireside
Simon & Schuster Building
Rockefeller Center
1230 Avenue of the Americas
New York, New York 10020

Copyright © 1991 by Lamppost Press, Inc.

Designed by Hedgerow Design
Manufactured in the United States of America

10   9   8   7   6   5   4   3   2   1

Library of Congress Cataloging in Publication Data
Moore, Sharon.
* Brownies/Sharon Moore.*
*   p.   cm.*
* "A Fireside book."*
* 1. Brownies (Cookery)   I. Title.*
TX771.M785   1991
641.8'653 — dc20   90-20456
*   CIP*

ISBN 0-671-69504-5

To my mother,
Avis Marie Stewart Freeman,
and to David and Ian

Contents

Chapter 3: Unexpected Brownies

Chapter 4: Sumptuous Brownies

Chapter 5: Blondies

Chapter 6: Healthy Brownies

Chapter 7: International Brownies

Chapter 8: The Brownie Controversy: Fudgy versus Cakelike

Chapter 9: Frostings and Toppings for Brownies

Chapter 10: How to Build a Brownie House

Introduction: Brownie History

*T*here is no recorded historical account of the brownie until an American legend was born in the eighteenth or nineteenth century: A story of Yankee practicality and know-how, it concerns a family cook whose chocolate cake fell flat. Either the unreliable wood-burning stove was at fault or the leavening agent failed (as often happened before baking powders were standardized in this century). Somehow the cake came out flat and heavy, but since chocolate was so expensive, the cautious chef set the cake aside to cool before throwing it out. Later, tasting it, she (or he) discovered that it was rich, moist and rather chewy, a cross between cake, cookie and candy. True, it was flat, but it looked appetizing enough and certainly tasted wonderful. So the chef cut the cake into squares and served it as a snack to the great delight of all the members of the household, who afterwards begged for repeats of the delicious "disaster."

How the flat, unrisen chocolate cake came to be called a brownie is unknown, but the term first appeared in print in the 1897 Sears, Roebuck and Co. catalog. Though the originator of the dish was not identified, its fame was established upon its debut in that annual arbiter of American taste.

Today the popularity of the brownie rivals that of chocolate-chip cookies. And even those who favor brownies disagree about their ideal consistency. Right from the beginning there was a controversy over whether brownies should be cakelike and light, or denser, more cookie-like and chewy. Some said that if the brownie was meant to be moist, it would be made like a Sacher torte, while others maintain that if it was meant to be a cookie, it would have chocolate chips.

The essential difference between cakelike and chewy brownies is the number of eggs used and the way the eggs are treated. For a lighter texture, using more well-beaten eggs is the secret. Using fewer eggs, beaten just enough for easy mixing, results in a firmer brownie. Recipes for cakelike brownies usually incorporate more leavening (baking powder or baking soda) than denser brownies. Thin, flatter brownies (less batter spread over a larger pan) tend to be chewier, while more batter in a smaller pan usually produces a lighter, cakelike brownie.

You will have to make up your own mind as to whether you prefer the moist or the chewy variety. Because we love all brownies, we've included both types of recipes, along with some brownies that are almost like pudding and some that resemble candy.

Brownies seem to lend themselves to almost any flavoring. The recipes in this book include ingredients as diverse as carrots, brandy, mint, pineapple, oatmeal and pepper.

HINTS

Here are some general baking tips to remember when making the brownie recipes that follow.

CHOCOLATE

What *is* chocolate? Which should you use — milk chocolate or bittersweet? Is white chocolate really chocolate?

All chocolate is derived from the beans of the tropical cacao tree. The beans are harvested and ground into a thick, rich chocolate liquor that contains about 53 percent cocoa butter. From this, various commercial chocolate products are made:

Semisweet or bittersweet chocolate contains at least 35 percent chocolate liquor mixed with sweeteners and cocoa butter.

Sweet chocolate consists of 15 percent chocolate liquor with sweeteners and cocoa butter.

White chocolate contains no chocolate liquor. It is made of white cocoa butter with milk products, sweeteners and such flavorings as vanilla.

Chocolate chips are made of unsweetened chocolate, sugar and cocoa butter.

Cocoa powder is the soft brown powder left when most of the cocoa butter is removed from chocolate liquor. The most popular kind of cocoa contains 10 to 22 percent cocoa butter. When it is treated with a mild alkali such as baking soda, its flavor is modified and its color is darkened; this is called dutched cocoa.

Mexican chocolate is available in specialty stores in large cities and in areas with large populations of Mexican-Americans. It consists of cocoa beans ground with almonds and sugar and formed into wafers. This was the chocolate of our pre-Columbian ancestors, though they restricted its use to the upper classes and often mixed their chocolate with honey or flower petals.

A basic cooking rule applies to the selection of chocolate: Always choose the best ingredients. The purest chocolate makes the best brownies. Noninstant cocoa powder produces a richer flavor than the more processed kind. Any brand of chocolate can be used in the amounts specified in the following recipes, but when a certain type of chocolate is called for, do follow the recommendation.

Chunk chocolate should be broken or chopped into 1- or 2-inch square pieces and melted slowly in a double boiler over hot water (not boiling) or in a small heavy pan over low heat. Some cooks add a teaspoon or two of water to the chocolate, if melting it without any butter, to avoid burning it and ruining the flavor. Stir melting chocolate frequently. Let the melted chocolate cool slightly, for about 10 to 15 minutes. It should not be hot enough to cook the ingredients it's added to, such as eggs, or the result will be dry and heavy brownies.

PREPARING THE PAN

Unless you are using a nonstick pan, butter the pan thoroughly. For heavy, fudgy-type brownies, you may be advised to line the pan with waxed paper: set the pan on top of the waxed paper and draw around it with a pencil. Cut out the waxed paper square with scissors, cutting inside the pencil line. Press the waxed paper down on the bottom of the buttered pan, and butter the paper. To flour the pan, sprinkle a tablespoon of flour around the buttered pan. Shake the pan and tilt it to coat the sides evenly with the flour. Then turn the pan upside down (over a garbage bag or the sink) and tap it to rid it of excess flour.

MIXING

Beat the eggs until they are foamy and pale yellow. Then gradually beat in the sugar and flavorings such as vanilla extract, salt, etc., until the batter nearly doubles in volume and falls from the beater in a thick ribbon. Avoid overbeating after this point. Then stir in the chocolate mixture.

INGREDIENTS

One-half cup of butter equals one stick or 8 tablespoons. Sugar means granulated sugar, unless another type of sugar is specified (e.g., light or dark brown sugar).

FLOUR

All-purpose flour is presifted. Sifting flour makes the finished product slightly lighter and more uniform, but it is not essential. I use un-bleached, unsifted white flour with wheat germ for baking, and I usually return the particles sifted out (mostly wheat germ) to the flour, to conserve valuable nutrients. Stir in the flour after the wet ingredients have been added, and before the flour is completely integrated, add the nuts or other solid flavorings (dried fruit, coconut, etc.) to avoid overmixing.

CITRUS ZEST

To produce the citrus zest called for in several of the recipes, rub the skin of the fruit against a grater until the white inner peel begins to show. Only the outside of the peel is called the zest, as it contains the desired flavoring.

BAKING

Pour the batter in the prepared pan and spread it evenly with a spatula. Place the pan on a rack set in the center of the oven. Test the baked brownies with a cake tester (a long wire with a loop at one end) or a toothpick or knife inserted into the center of the pan; if it comes out clean or nearly clean (see individual recipes), the batch is done. Do not overbake brownies or the chocolate will not remain moist.

Set the pan on a wire rack to cool for 10 minutes, then remove the brownies: run a sharp knife around the sides of the pan, place a plate facedown on top of the pan, and invert plate and pan together. Tap the bottom of the pan to loosen the brownies, then remove the pan. Cool the plate of brownies on the wire rack for 10 minutes or more. Using a sharp knife dipped in cold water, cut the brownies into 2-inch squares. (Refrigerated brownies cut more easily.) You may cut them into squares while they are still in the pan, but use a plastic cutting tool if the brownies were baked in a vegetable-oil-coated nonstick pan. An 8-inch pan yields sixteen 2-inch square brownies.

MICROWAVING

To bake brownies in a microwave oven, cover the corners of a square microwaveable pan smoothly with foil, or use a round microwaveable pan. Place the pan on top of a small, inverted microwaveable bowl. For a roughly 8-inch square pan, cook on medium for about 8 minutes, then remove the foil from the corners of the pan. Cook on high for an additional 1 to 5 minutes, until firm on top and/or a cake tester comes out nearly clean.

GARNISHING

Most brownies are served just as they come out of the oven, crisp and brown and unadorned. However, special effects are always exciting. Many of the recipes that follow include special toppings, but you may wish to consider the following decorations.

FROSTING

When the brownies have cooled slightly on a wire rack, place them on a plate. Using a table knife, spread frosting evenly over top (and sides, too, if you wish). Use the knife to make swirls and flourishes in the frosting before it sets. Then cut the brownies into squares.

LACE

When the brownies have cooled slightly, place them on a plate and lay a paper doily over them. Press down slightly. Sprinkle confectioners' sugar evenly over the doily. Carefully lift the doily straight up and move it away quickly. Cut the brownies into squares with a damp knife.

CURLS

Shave thin parings off chunk chocolate with a vegetable peeler or knife, or use a chocolate grater. Sprinkle curls over the top of cooled brownies.

CHOCOLATE-DIPPED FRUIT

Melt 2 ounces of bittersweet chocolate in a double boiler over hot water or in a heavy pan over low heat. Beat until cool enough to be touched with your hand. Into the chocolate, dip whole strawberries, cherries, raspberries, slices of kiwi fruit, pineapple chunks or dried apricots, skewered on toothpicks or held by the stem. Use only perfect fruits. Place the dipped fruits on waxed paper and chill until the chocolate is set and shiny. It may be necessary to return the chocolate to low heat if it solidifies before you have finished dipping.

The Ten Best Brownie Recipes Ever

Elegant, aromatically chocolate, richly moist and chewy, these brownies share the simplicity and directness of the true American brownie, yet each offers its own special pleasures.

The Ultimate Brownie

*Classically bittersweet,
pure and sensuous, this is
the definitive brownie.*

4 OUNCES UNSWEETENED CHOCOLATE
1/2 CUP BUTTER
2 LARGE EGGS
1 1/2 CUP SUGAR
1 TEASPOON VANILLA EXTRACT
1/2 CUP ALL-PURPOSE FLOUR
1/4 TEASPOON SALT
1 CUP CHOPPED WALNUTS OR PECANS

1. Preheat the oven to 350°F.
2. Butter and flour an 8-inch square baking pan.
3. Melt the chocolate and butter in a double boiler over hot water or in a heavy pan over low heat, stirring occasionally; let cool slightly.
4. In a large mixing bowl, beat the eggs, gradually adding the sugar. Beat until just combined, scraping down the sides of the bowl as needed. Add the chocolate mixture and vanilla, and stir in the flour and salt until just blended. Fold in nuts.
5. Spread evenly in the prepared pan. Bake 20 to 25 minutes. Cool completely in the pan and cut into squares.

Chocolate Iced Brownies

How to make a sinfully rich brownie even better: add more chocolate on top!

14 OUNCES BITTERSWEET CHOCOLATE, DIVIDED

6 TABLESPOONS UNSALTED BUTTER

1 CUP SUGAR

3 LARGE EGGS

3/4 CUP ALL-PURPOSE FLOUR

1. Preheat oven to 325°F.
2. Butter an 8 × 12-inch pan and line the bottom with waxed paper. Then butter the paper and flour the pan.
3. Melt 8 ounces of the chocolate in the top of a double boiler over hot water or in a heavy pan. Let cool slightly.
4. In a large mixing bowl, cream the butter and sugar until very smooth. Add the eggs and beat for 2 minutes. Add the melted chocolate and fold in the flour. Mix only until smooth; do not overbeat.
5. Pour the batter into the prepared pan and bake about 30 minutes, until firm on top and/or a cake tester or toothpick comes out clean.
6. Grate the remaining chocolate and sprinkle over the brownies immediately after removing them from the oven. As it melts, spread the chocolate topping evenly over the brownies. When cooled, cut into squares.

Ganache Brownies

*Bittersweet brownies
topped with a rich
French frosting.*

6 OUNCES BITTERSWEET CHOCOLATE
1/2 CUP UNSALTED BUTTER
2 LARGE EGGS
1 CUP SUGAR
1 TEASPOON VANILLA EXTRACT
3/4 CUP ALL-PURPOSE FLOUR
1/2 TEASPOON BAKING POWDER
1/4 TEASPOON SALT
1/2 CUP CHOPPED WALNUTS
7 OUNCES SEMISWEET CHOCOLATE
1/2 CUP HEAVY CREAM

1. Preheat the oven to 350°F.
2. Butter a 9-inch square pan. Line the bottom with waxed paper and butter the paper. Flour the pan.
3. Melt the bittersweet chocolate and butter in a heavy pan over low heat or in a double boiler over hot water. Cool slightly.
4. In a large mixing bowl, beat the eggs until uniformly yellow. Beat in sugar until thick. Add vanilla. Add chocolate gradually. Sift together flour, baking powder and salt and add to chocolate mixture. Fold in the walnuts.

5. Scrape the batter into the prepared pan and spread evenly. Bake about 35 minutes until firm and/or a cake tester comes out clean.
6. Cool in the pan for ten minutes, then remove the brownies and place them on a plate.
7. Chop the semisweet chocolate fine and place in a small heatproof bowl. Slowly bring the cream to a full boil in a small saucepan, stirring frequently. Pour it over the chocolate and whisk until the chocolate is melted and the mixture is smooth. Chill briefly until thickened, about 15 minutes. Spread over the brownies and let cool until a glaze forms on top. Cut brownies into squares.

Basic Brownies

Your standard brownie, rich and chocolaty — can't be beat!

5 OUNCES UNSWEETENED CHOCOLATE
1/2 CUP UNSALTED BUTTER
4 LARGE EGGS
2 CUPS SUGAR
1 TEASPOON VANILLA EXTRACT
1 CUP ALL-PURPOSE FLOUR
1/4 TEASPOON SALT
1 CUP CHOPPED WALNUTS

1. Preheat the oven to 350°F.
2. Butter a 9-inch square baking pan.
3. Melt the chocolate and butter in a double boiler over hot water or in a heavy pan over a low flame. Let cool.
4. In a large mixing bowl, beat the eggs until light and foamy. Beat in the sugar and vanilla until well creamed. Blend in the chocolate mixture. Fold in the flour, salt and walnuts.
5. Pour into the prepared pan and bake for about 25 minutes. Cool before cutting into squares.

Chocolate-on-Chocolate Brownies

A double dose of that delectable delicacy.

8 OUNCES UNSWEETENED CHOCOLATE, DIVIDED
¾ CUP UNSALTED BUTTER
3 LARGE EGGS
2 CUPS SUGAR
1 TEASPOON VANILLA EXTRACT
1 CUP ALL-PURPOSE FLOUR
¼ TEASPOON SALT
1 CUP CHOPPED WALNUTS, DIVIDED
1 TABLESPOON WATER

1. Preheat the oven to 350°F.
2. Butter and flour a 9-inch square pan.
3. Melt 6 ounces of the chocolate with the butter in a double boiler over hot water or in a heavy pan over low heat. Let cool.
4. In a large mixing bowl, beat the eggs until lemon-yellow and frothy, then add the sugar a little at a time while continuing to beat until the mixture is light-colored and thick. Stir in the choco-

late mixture and vanilla. Sift the flour with the salt and stir into the egg-chocolate mixture. Blend well and stir in $3/4$ cup of the nuts.

5. Spread the batter evenly in the prepared pan and bake for about 35 minutes, until firm to the touch and/or a cake tester comes out clean.

6. Melt the remaining 2 ounces of chocolate with the water in the same pan previously used for melting chocolate. Stir in the remaining $1/4$ cup nuts. Refrigerate this mixture about 15 minutes. Remove the brownies from the pan and place them on a plate. Spread the cooled chocolate-nut topping on the brownies. Let cool (or refrigerate for faster cooling) before cutting into squares.

Chocolate Chip Brownies

A whiff of cinnamon adds piquance to these delicious squares.

1 CUP SUGAR
3/4 CUP UNSALTED BUTTER
2 LARGE EGGS
1 TEASPOON VANILLA EXTRACT
2 CUPS ALL-PURPOSE FLOUR
1/4 TEASPOON BAKING POWDER
1/2 TEASPOON SALT
1/2 TEASPOON CINNAMON
6 OUNCES SEMISWEET CHOCOLATE BITS
1/2 CUP CHOPPED WALNUTS OR PECANS

1. Preheat the oven to 350°F.
2. Butter a 9 × 13-inch square pan.
3. In a large mixing bowl, beat the sugar and butter together until fluffy. Beat in the eggs one at a time. Add the vanilla.
4. Sift the flour, baking powder, salt and cinnamon together. Stir into the batter. Fold in the chocolate bits and nuts.
5. Scrape the batter into the prepared pan and spread it evenly. Bake for about 35 minutes, until firm on top and/or a cake tester comes out clean. Cool before cutting into squares.

Brownie Tarte

*Two — count 'em, two —
layers of chocolate
goodness. Simply superb!*

10 OUNCES BITTERSWEET CHOCOLATE,
DIVIDED
1/2 CUP PLUS 1 TABLESPOON UNSALTED
BUTTER, DIVIDED
3/4 CUP UNSWEETENED COCOA
3 LARGE EGGS
2 CUPS SUGAR, DIVIDED
1/2 TEASPOON VANILLA EXTRACT
1 CUP ALL-PURPOSE FLOUR
1 CUP CHOPPED WALNUTS OR PECANS
1/2 CUP HEAVY CREAM

1. Preheat the oven to 375°F.
2. Butter a 9-inch square pan. Line it with waxed paper, then butter the paper. Flour the pan.
3. Melt 2 ounces of the chocolate and 1/2 cup of the butter in a double boiler over hot water or in a heavy pan over low heat. Sift the cocoa and add it to the chocolate, stirring well until the mixture is smooth. Let cool slightly.
4. In a large mixing bowl, beat the eggs and 1 3/4 cups of the sugar until thickened and light-colored. Add the chocolate mixture and

the vanilla and beat just until smooth. Sift the flour and fold it into the egg-chocolate mixture, adding the nuts.

5. Spread the mixture evenly in the prepared pan and bake for about 35 minutes, or until a cake tester comes out with crumbs on it. Cool in the pan. Then remove from the pan and place brownies on a plate, still uncut.

6. Chop the remaining 8 ounces of chocolate fine. Place it in a small heatproof bowl. Combine the cream, the remaining 1 tablespoon butter and the remaining ¼ cup sugar in a saucepan and bring slowly to a boil. Pour the cream mixture over the chopped chocolate and whisk briskly until the chocolate is melted and the mixture smooth. Let stand for 5 or 10 minutes until thickened and pour over the brownie, spreading the topping evenly. Cool until the topping forms a glaze, then cut into squares.

Butterfudge Delights

A triple treat—brownies topped with a chocolate frosting plus a chocolate glaze.

6 OUNCES UNSWEETENED CHOCOLATE, DIVIDED

¾ CUP UNSALTED BUTTER, DIVIDED

2 LARGE EGGS

1 CUP SUGAR

FEW DROPS ALMOND EXTRACT

½ CUP ALL-PURPOSE FLOUR

½ TEASPOON SALT

1 ½ CUPS CONFECTIONERS' SUGAR

¼ CUP HEAVY CREAM

½ TEASPOON VANILLA EXTRACT

¼ CUP CHOPPED ALMONDS

1. Preheat oven to 350°F.
2. Butter and flour a 9-inch square baking pan.
3. Melt 2 ounces of the chocolate and ½ cup of the butter in a double boiler over hot water or in a heavy pan over low heat. Let cool.
4. In a large mixing bowl, beat the eggs until lemon-colored and frothy. Gradually add the sugar, then beat until light and fluffy. Gradually add the chocolate mixture and almond extract. Stir in flour and salt until just blended.

5. Spread evenly in the prepared pan and bake for 30 minutes, or until a cake tester comes out almost clean. Cool.
6. For the frosting, melt 2 ounces of the chocolate and 3 tablespoons butter in the double boiler or heavy pan until it bubbles. Combine the chocolate-butter mixture and confectioners' sugar in a mixing bowl and beat until smooth. Gradually add the cream and vanilla and beat until smooth and creamy. Spread the frosting on the baked brownies. Refrigerate until firm.
7. For the glaze, melt 2 ounces of the chocolate with the remaining tablespoon of butter. Cool slightly and spread over the brownies and frosting. Sprinkle with chopped nuts. Let cool, then remove carefully from the pan and cut into squares.

Serendipity Brownies with Six Variations

In a legend of ancient India, the princes of Serendip had a knack for discovering wondrous things while trekking about. They might've discovered these brownies if they were trekking through a variety of kitchens!

4 OUNCES UNSWEETENED CHOCOLATE
½ CUP UNSALTED BUTTER
2 LARGE EGGS
1½ CUPS SUGAR
½ TEASPOON VANILLA EXTRACT
½ CUP ALL-PURPOSE FLOUR
¼ TEASPOON SALT

1. Preheat the oven to 350°F.
2. Butter and flour an 8-inch square baking pan.
3. Melt the chocolate and butter in a double boiler over hot water or in a heavy pan over low heat. Let cool slightly.
4. In a large mixing bowl, beat the eggs until pale and foamy. Gradually add the sugar and beat until light and fluffy. Beat in the chocolate mixture and vanilla. Stir in the flour and salt until just combined.

5. Spread the mixture evenly in the prepared pan and bake about 30 minutes or until a cake tester comes out almost clean. Cool and cut into squares.

Variation 1: Fold in 1 cup chopped peanuts, walnuts or almonds into the batter after adding the flour.

Variation 2: Reduce the amount of flour to ¼ cup and add ⅓ cup oat bran.

Variation 3: Fold in ½ cup chopped raisins, dates, figs, apricots or candied citron after adding the flour.

Variation 4: Fold in ½ cup semisweet chocolate bits after adding the flour.

Variation 5: Substitute ¼ cup brandy or your favorite liqueur for the vanilla.

Variation 6: Add ½ teaspoon chopped dried orange rind, ½ teaspoon cinnamon and ¼ teaspoon cloves along with the flour in step 4.

German's Chocolate Brownies

German's is a sweet
chocolate that was
created by an American
baker, Samuel German,
in 1851. It is usually
used in a rich cake with
a coconut-pecan frosting.
It can be found wherever
baking chocolate is sold.

4 OUNCES GERMAN'S SWEET CHOCOLATE
6 TABLESPOONS UNSALTED BUTTER
3 OUNCES CREAM CHEESE
1 CUP SUGAR
3 LARGE EGGS
1/2 CUP PLUS 1 TABLESPOON ALL-PURPOSE
FLOUR, DIVIDED
1 TEASPOON VANILLA EXTRACT
1/2 TEASPOON BAKING POWDER
1/4 TEASPOON SALT
1/4 TEASPOON ALMOND EXTRACT
(OPTIONAL)
1/2 CUP CHOPPED PECANS
1/2 CUP SHREDDED COCONUT

1. Preheat the oven to 350°F.
2. Butter and flour a 9-inch baking pan.
3. Melt the chocolate and 2 tablespoons of the butter in a double
   boiler over hot water or in a heavy pan over a low flame. Let cool.
4. In a medium mixing bowl, cream the remaining butter with the
   cream cheese. Gradually add 1/4 cup sugar and beat until fluffy.
   Add 1 egg, 1 tablespoon of the flour and 1/2 teaspoon vanilla. Mix
   well.

5. In another large mixing bowl, beat 2 eggs until thick and lemon-colored. Gradually add ¾ cup sugar and beat until thick. Stir in the remaining ½ cup flour and the baking powder and salt. To this add the chocolate mixture, ½ teaspoon vanilla, almond extract (if desired), pecans and coconut.
6. Spread half the chocolate mixture evenly in the prepared pan. Top with the cream-cheese mixture, then the remaining half of the chocolate batter. Use a sharp knife to cut zigzags through all three layers, creating a marble effect. Bake about 35 minutes. Let cool, then cut into squares.

Fruity and Nutty Brownies

Many fruits and most nuts enhance the taste of chocolate and lend textural interest to the basic brownie. Here are some classics and some funky new combinations.

Almond Brownies

Subtle and sophisticated, this is a dessert to savor at length.

I CUP ALMOND PASTE AT ROOM
TEMPERATURE
2 OUNCES UNSWEETENED CHOCOLATE
2 CUPS SUGAR
I CUP BUTTER AT ROOM TEMPERATURE
3 LARGE EGGS
2 TEASPOONS VANILLA EXTRACT
I CUP ALL-PURPOSE FLOUR
$1/4$ TEASPOON BAKING POWDER
I CUP CHOPPED TOASTED ALMONDS
4 OUNCES SEMISWEET CHOCOLATE

1. Preheat the oven to 325°F.
2. Butter and flour a 9 × 13-inch baking pan.
3. Place the almond paste on a piece of waxed paper approximately 20 inches long. Place another piece of waxed paper the same size on top and roll the almond paste out between them into a 9 × 13-inch rectangle. Set aside.
4. Melt the unsweetened chocolate in a double boiler over hot water or in a heavy pan over a low flame. Let cool.
5. In a large mixing bowl, cream the sugar and butter together. Add

the eggs one at a time, beating well after each addition. Beat in the melted chocolate and vanilla, then stir in the flour and baking powder. Fold in the almonds.

6. Scrape half the batter into the prepared pan and spread it evenly. Top with the layer of almond paste. Spread the remaining batter over the almond paste. Bake approximately 45 minutes. Let cool.

7. Melt the semisweet chocolate in a double boiler or heavy pan over low flame. Let it cool slightly, then spread it over the brownies. Cut into squares.

Pistachio Brownies

Deep dark brownies with the color and crunch of pistachio nuts.

6 OUNCES UNSWEETENED CHOCOLATE
1 CUP PLUS 2 TABLESPOONS BUTTER AT
ROOM TEMPERATURE
¾ CUP GRANULATED SUGAR
¾ CUP FIRMLY PACKED DARK BROWN SUGAR
3 LARGE EGGS
½ TEASPOON VANILLA EXTRACT
1 CUP ALL-PURPOSE FLOUR
¼ TEASPOON SALT
¼ CUP CHOPPED PISTACHIO NUTS

1. Preheat the oven to 375°F.
2. Butter and flour a 9-inch square baking pan.
3. Melt 4 ounces of the chocolate in a double boiler over hot water or in a heavy pan over low heat. Let cool.
4. In a large mixing bowl, cream 1 cup of the butter and the sugars together until light-colored and fluffy. Add the eggs one at a time, beating well after each addition. Add the melted chocolate and the vanilla. Stir in the flour and salt.
5. Spread evenly in the prepared pan and bake about 30 minutes or until top is firm and/or a cake tester comes out clean. Let cool.
6. Melt the remaining chocolate and butter in a double boiler or heavy pan previously used. Let cool about 15 minutes, then spread over the brownies and immediately sprinkle the pistachio nuts over the glaze. Let cool until glaze becomes shiny. Cut into squares.

Chocolate Pine Nut Bars

Easy to make in a food processor, these brownies are mysterious with the dark, sweet tastes of raspberry and chocolate, accented with the richness of toasted pine nuts.

2 LARGE EGGS
½ CUP PLUS 2 TABLESPOONS SUGAR
¼ TEASPOON SALT
2 TEASPOONS VANILLA EXTRACT
2 TEASPOONS GRATED LEMON ZEST
I CUP UNSALTED BUTTER, CHILLED
2 CUPS ALL-PURPOSE FLOUR, SIFTED
(DIVIDED)
I CUP PINE NUTS
½ CUP RASPBERRY JAM
6 OUNCES SEMISWEET CHOCOLATE BITS

1. Blend the eggs, ½ cup sugar, salt, vanilla, lemon zest and butter in a food processor. Pulse about 12 times, then process continuously for 5 seconds. Add 1¾ cup of the flour and ½ cup of the pine nuts and process about 2 seconds. Scrape down the sides of the container and process a few seconds more until crumbly. Scrape out dough, form into a ball, wrap in plastic wrap and refrigerate about 1 hour.
2. Preheat the oven to 350°F.
3. Butter and flour a 9 × 13-inch baking pan.

4. Remove a fourth of the dough and reserve. Roll out the remainder into a 9 × 13-inch rectangle. Press it evenly into the pan.
5. Spread the remaining ½ cup pine nuts in a single layer in a flat pan and toast in the preheated 350°F. oven, shaking the pan occasionally, for about 15 minutes, or until lightly browned. Cool slightly.
6. Spread the jam gently over the dough in the pan, leaving a ¼-inch margin around the edges. Sprinkle the pine nuts and chocolate bits evenly over the jam.
7. Cut the reserved dough into 12 cubes and place them in the (cleaned) food processor. Add the remaining 2 tablespoons sugar and ¼ cup flour and pulse a few times until blended but crumbly. Sprinkle the crumbs evenly over the jam topping.
8. Bake about 30 minutes until the crumbly topping is light brown and firm. Cool and cut into squares.

Go Nuts Brownies

*If you just can't get
enough hazelnuts, you'll
get a rise out of these
brownies—the nuts come
up to the surface during
baking. If you can't find
hazelnuts on the market,
substitute their American
cousin the filbert, or
pecans.*

2 CUPS WHOLE HAZELNUTS
½ CUP BUTTER
1 CUP SUGAR
¼ CUP UNSWEETENED COCOA
2 TEASPOONS VANILLA EXTRACT
2 LARGE EGGS, LIGHTLY BEATEN
½ CUP ALL-PURPOSE FLOUR

1. Preheat the oven to 350°F.
2. Butter and flour a 9-inch square baking pan.
3. Spread the hazelnuts evenly in a flat pan and toast them in the
   preheated 350°F. oven, shaking the pan occasionally, for about 20
   minutes, or until lightly browned. Remove hazelnut skins by rub-
   bing them. Cool completely and chop coarsely.
4. In a heavy pan, melt the butter over low heat. Stir in the sugar,
   cocoa and vanilla. Let cool. Blend in the eggs thoroughly. Stir in
   the flour until mixture is well streaked, then add nuts and continue
   stirring until completely blended.

5. Pour into the prepared pan and bake about 25 minutes or until the brownies begin to pull away from the sides of the pan. Cool and cut into squares.

Pecan Date Squares

Unbelievably light and delectable, these are worth the extra trouble required!

4 OUNCES UNSWEETENED CHOCOLATE
1 TABLESPOON WATER
1/2 CUP UNSALTED BUTTER AT ROOM TEMPERATURE
2 CUPS SUGAR, DIVIDED
3 LARGE EGGS, SEPARATED
1 TEASPOON VANILLA EXTRACT
1 CUP CAKE FLOUR
1 CUP PLUS 1 TABLESPOON ALL-PURPOSE FLOUR
2 TEASPOONS BAKING POWDER
1/2 TEASPOON SALT
1 CUP MILK
2 CUPS CHOPPED DATES
2 CUPS CHOPPED PECANS

1. Preheat the oven to 350°F.
2. Butter and flour a 9 × 13-inch baking pan.
3. Melt the chocolate with the water in a double boiler over hot water or in a heavy pan over low heat. Let cool.
4. In a large mixing bowl, cream the butter with 1¾ cups of the sugar until light and fluffy. Beat in the 3 egg yolks one at a time, beating well after each addition. Beat in the chocolate and vanilla.
5. Sift together the two flours (reserving 1 tablespoon of the all-purpose flour), baking powder and salt. Add gradually to the chocolate mixture alternately with the milk. Beat until very light and fluffy.
6. Toss the dates with 1 tablespoon all-purpose flour and fold them and the pecans into the batter.
7. In another mixing bowl, beat the egg whites until they form stiff peaks. Gradually beat in the remaining ¼ cup sugar. Fold the egg-white mixture into the batter gently.
8. Pour into the prepared pan and bake about 30 minutes until the top is firm and/or a cake tester comes out clean.

Chestnut Fudgies

Chestnuts — whose flavor evokes the spirit of the Christmas holidays for many people — add a whole new dimension to chocolate. This is one of my personal favorites.

½ POUND RAW CHESTNUTS
1 TABLESPOON OLIVE OIL
5 OUNCES SEMISWEET CHOCOLATE
6 TABLESPOONS UNSALTED BUTTER
2 LARGE EGGS
1 CUP SUGAR
1 TEASPOON VANILLA EXTRACT
2 TABLESPOONS COGNAC
½ CUP PLUS 1 TABLESPOON ALL-PURPOSE FLOUR
¼ TEASPOON SALT

1. Preheat the oven to 350°F.
2. Butter an 8-inch square pan. Line the base and sides with waxed paper, then butter the paper.
3. Slash an X on the flat side of each chestnut with a sharp knife. Place them in a small baking pan with 1 tablespoon olive oil and heat on top of the stove until they begin to sizzle. In the same pan, bake in the oven about 20 to 30 minutes, until the slashed peel has begun to curl back. Remove and cool. Peel the chestnuts, removing any stubborn inner skins with a knife. Chop the chestnuts coarsely.

4. Melt the chocolate and butter in a double boiler over hot water or in a heavy pan over low heat. Let cool.
5. In a large mixing bowl, beat the eggs until lemon-colored and frothy. Beat in the sugar. Add the chocolate mixture, vanilla and cognac, beating well. Sift the flour and salt and stir into the batter, then stir in the chestnuts.
6. Spread the batter evenly in the prepared pan and bake for about 30 minutes, until the top is firm and/or a cake tester comes out nearly clean. Cool and cut into squares.

Praline Brownies

The traditional southern flavor created with sugar, butter and pecans lends itself remarkably well to brownies.

4 OUNCES UNSWEETENED CHOCOLATE
I CUP GRANULATED SUGAR
I CUP FIRMLY PACKED DARK BROWN SUGAR
1/2 CUP UNSALTED BUTTER AT ROOM TEMPERATURE
3 LARGE EGGS
I CUP ALL-PURPOSE FLOUR
1/2 TEASPOON SALT
I CUP PECAN HALVES

1. Preheat the oven to 350°F.
2. Butter and flour a 9-inch square baking pan.
3. Melt the chocolate in a double boiler over hot water or in a heavy pan over a low flame. Cool.
4. In a large mixing bowl, beat together the sugars and the butter until smooth and creamy. Add the eggs one at a time, beating well after each addition. Stir in the chocolate. Sift together the flour and salt, and stir it into the chocolate mixture. Reserving 16 of the pecan halves to decorate the brownies, chop the remaining pecans and stir into the batter.
5. Spread the batter evenly in the prepared pan and place the reserved pecan halves on top, in four rows of four. Bake for about 35 minutes, until the top is firm and the batter pulls slightly away from the pan, and/or a cake tester comes out clean. Cool and cut into 16 squares.

Banana Split Brownies

Kid food for children of all ages! If these brownies aren't hedonistic enough for you, serve them with split bananas, ice cream and hot fudge sauce!

4 OUNCES UNSWEETENED CHOCOLATE
1/2 CUP BUTTER
2 LARGE EGGS
1 1/2 CUPS SUGAR
1 TEASPOON VANILLA EXTRACT
3/4 CUP ALL-PURPOSE FLOUR
1/4 TEASPOON BAKING POWDER
1/4 TEASPOON SALT
1 CUP MASHED BANANAS
(2 OR 3 BANANAS)*
1/2 CUP DRIED BANANA CHIPS (OPTIONAL —
INTENSIFIES THE BANANA FLAVOR AND
ADDS CRUNCH.)

1. Preheat the oven to 350°F.
2. Butter and flour an 8-inch square baking pan.
3. Melt the chocolate and butter together in a double boiler over hot water or in a heavy pan over low heat. Cool.

* Very ripe bananas mash best and have the most flavor.

4. In a large mixing bowl, beat the eggs, gradually adding the sugar, until thick and smooth. Beat in the chocolate mixture and vanilla.

5. Sift together the flour, baking powder and salt. Add the flour mixture alternately with the bananas, beating gently after each addition. Stir in the banana chips (if desired). Spread the batter evenly in the prepared pan and bake about 25 minutes, until firm on top and/or a cake tester comes out nearly clean. Cool and cut into squares.

Unexpected Brownies

Everything but the kitchen sink! Well, almost everything . . .

Rocky Road Brownies

Quick and easy indulgence, with no chocolate to melt! You can vary these by adding any treat that turns you on — shredded coconut, M&Ms, colored sprinkles, crushed cookies, raisins, etc. — in small amounts (¹/₄ cup), or in place of some of the topping ingredients listed below.

1 ¼ CUP ALL-PURPOSE FLOUR
¹/₄ TEASPOON BAKING POWDER
¹/₄ TEASPOON SALT
1 LARGE EGG
¹/₃ CUP SUGAR
¹/₂ CUP CHOCOLATE SYRUP
¹/₂ TEASPOON VANILLA EXTRACT
1 TABLESPOON MELTED BUTTER
1 CUP MINIATURE MARSHMALLOWS
¹/₂ CUP CHOPPED WALNUTS OR PECANS
1 CUP SEMISWEET CHOCOLATE BITS

1. Preheat the oven to 350°F.
2. Butter an 8-inch square baking pan.
3. Sift together the flour, baking powder and salt. In a separate large mixing bowl beat the egg until foamy. Add sugar, chocolate syrup and vanilla to egg and beat just to mix. Stir in the butter, then the flour mixture.

4. Spread evenly in the pan. Bake 25 minutes, or until the top springs back when pressed.
5. Remove cake from the oven and immediately sprinkle it with the marshmallows, walnuts and chocolate bits (and/or any toppings you crave). Return to the oven for 2 or 3 minutes until the chocolate bits are softened but marshmallows are not melted. With the back of a spoon, spread the chocolate lightly over the marshmallows, nuts and any other toppings. Cool and cut into squares.

Yellow Brick Road Brownies

Made from scratch, with no shortcuts. The way Aunt Em would've made them.

3 OUNCES UNSWEETENED CHOCOLATE, DIVIDED

½ CUP UNSALTED BUTTER, DIVIDED

2 LARGE EGGS

1 CUP SUGAR

½ TEASPOON VANILLA EXTRACT

½ CUP ALL-PURPOSE FLOUR

½ TEASPOON BAKING POWDER

¼ TEASPOON SALT

1 CUP CHOPPED WALNUTS OR PECANS, DIVIDED

2 DOZEN FULL-SIZE MARSHMALLOWS

1 CUP CONFECTIONERS' SUGAR

1 TABLESPOON BOILING WATER

½ CUP GOLDEN (SULTANA) RAISINS

1. Preheat the oven to 350°F.
2. Butter a 9 × 13-inch baking pan.
3. Melt 2 ounces of the chocolate and all but 1 tablespoon of the butter in a double boiler over hot water or in a heavy pan over low heat. Cool.
4. In a large mixing bowl, cream the eggs and sugar until light and

fluffy. Beat in the chocolate mixture and vanilla. Sift together the flour, baking powder and salt and stir them into the batter. Add half the nuts and blend gently but thoroughly.

5. Spread evenly in the prepared pan and bake about 25 minutes, until a cake tester comes out almost clean.

6. While the brownies are baking, cut the marshmallows in half with scissors dipped in cold water. Melt the remaining 1 ounce of chocolate and 1 tablespoon butter in the double boiler or heavy pan.

7. As soon as cake comes out of the oven, arrange the marshmallow halves evenly over it and return it to the oven for a minute, until the marshmallows soften.

8. Beat the confectioners' sugar and boiling water into the melted chocolate, adding more hot water as necessary to create a pourable glaze.

9. Sprinkle the remaining nuts and the raisins over the marshmallows and drizzle the glaze over the marshmallows. Cool thoroughly and cut carefully into squares.

Black Pepper Brownies

That once-exotic spice from the Orient, pepper, adds zest to chocolate in these unusually delicious brownies.

4 OUNCES UNSWEETENED CHOCOLATE
1/2 CUP UNSALTED BUTTER
2 LARGE EGGS
I CUP SUGAR
1/4 TEASPOON VANILLA EXTRACT
1/4 TEASPOON ALMOND EXTRACT
1/2 CUP ALL-PURPOSE FLOUR
1/4 TEASPOON SALT
1/2 TEASPOON BLACK PEPPER, PREFERABLY
FRESHLY GRATED
1/2 CUP CHOPPED ALMONDS

1. Preheat the oven to 350°F.
2. Butter an 8-inch baking pan and line it with waxed paper. Butter the waxed paper and flour the entire pan.
3. Melt the chocolate and butter in a double boiler over hot water or in a heavy pan over a low flame. Cool.
4. In a large mixing bowl, beat the eggs until lemon-colored and frothy. Beat in the sugar until thick and creamy. Beat in the chocolate mixture and the vanilla and almond extracts. Stir in the flour, salt and pepper, and fold in the almonds.

5. Spread evenly in the prepared pan and bake for about 40 minutes, until firm on top and/or a cake tester comes out nearly clean. Cool and cut into squares.

Strawberry Brownies

If you've ever savored the pleasures of chocolate-dipped strawberries, you'll understand the appeal of these brownies. You might want to garnish this batch with fresh, ripe strawberries dipped halfway into melted bittersweet chocolate.

2 1/2 CUPS ALL-PURPOSE FLOUR, DIVIDED
1 1/2 CUPS SUGAR, DIVIDED
1/2 TEASPOON BAKING POWDER
1/2 TEASPOON SALT, DIVIDED
1 CUP UNSALTED BUTTER AT ROOM
TEMPERATURE, DIVIDED
3 LARGE EGGS
3 TABLESPOONS UNSWEETENED COCOA
1 TEASPOON VANILLA EXTRACT
1 CUP STRAWBERRY PRESERVES

1. Preheat the oven to 350°F.
2. Prepare the pastry layer first. Combine 1¾ cups flour, ½ cup sugar,

baking powder and ¼ teaspoon salt in a mixing bowl and blend them with a fork, adding ½ cup of the butter, cut into pieces. Blend until the consistency of the mixture resembles small peas.

3. Add one lightly beaten egg and blend well until it forms a ball.

4. Press the dough into the bottom of an 8-inch square baking pan (unbuttered) and bake for about 20 minutes, or until a cake tester comes out clean, and set aside.

5. While the pastry is baking, melt the remaining ½ cup of butter in a butter melter or heavy pan over low heat. Place in a mixing bowl and stir the cocoa into it until blended. Stir in 1 cup of sugar. Add the remaining two eggs one at a time, beating well after each addition. Add the vanilla, the remaining ¾ cup of flour and ¼ teaspoon salt.

6. Spread the strawberry preserves evenly over the baked pastry layer. Carefully spread the chocolate mixture over the preserves, spreading it evenly but not mixing layers. Bake for about 25 minutes, or until a cake tester comes out clean. Cool and cut into squares.

Polar Brownies

Chocolate takes on a whole new life when refrigerated. These are a cool, refreshing summertime treat.

4 OUNCES UNSWEETENED CHOCOLATE
¾ CUP UNSALTED BUTTER
3 LARGE EGGS
2 CUPS SUGAR
1 TEASPOON VANILLA EXTRACT
1 CUP ALL-PURPOSE FLOUR
¼ TEASPOON SALT
½ CUP CHOPPED WALNUTS OR PECANS

1. Preheat the oven to 350°F.
2. Butter and flour a 9-inch square pan.
3. Melt the chocolate and butter in a double boiler over hot water or in a heavy pan over low heat. Cool.
4. In a large mixing bowl, beat the eggs until frothy and lemon-colored and beat in the sugar gradually until thick, creamy and smooth. Beat in the chocolate mixture and the vanilla. Stir in the flour and salt and add the nuts before the flour is completely incorporated.
5. Spread the batter evenly in the prepared pan and bake about 35 minutes, until it pulls away slightly from the sides of the pan and/ or a cake tester comes out almost clean. Chill in the refrigerator

several hours before removing from the pan and cutting into squares.

Serve cold. To keep cut brownies fresh in the refrigerator, wrap tightly in plastic wrap or foil.

Chocolate Mint Brownies

An after-dinner mint you can sink your teeth into — of course, you don't have to wait until after dinner!

3 OUNCES UNSWEETENED CHOCOLATE, DIVIDED
¾ CUP UNSALTED BUTTER, DIVIDED
2 LARGE EGGS
1 CUP SUGAR
½ TEASPOON VANILLA EXTRACT
½ CUP ALL-PURPOSE FLOUR
¼ TEASPOON SALT
1 CUP CONFECTIONERS' SUGAR
2 TABLESPOONS HEAVY CREAM
½ TEASPOON PEPPERMINT EXTRACT

1. Preheat the oven to 350°F.
2. Butter and flour an 8-inch square baking pan.

3. Melt 2 ounces of the chocolate and ½ cup of the butter in a double boiler over hot water or in a heavy pan over low heat. Cool.
4. In a large mixing bowl, beat the eggs until frothy. Beat in the sugar. Beat in the chocolate mixture and vanilla and blend well. Stir in the flour and salt to combine thoroughly.
5. Spread the mixture evenly in the prepared pan and bake about 30 minutes, until firm on top and/or a cake tester comes out almost clean. Cool slightly.
6. In a small mixing bowl, beat together 3 tablespoons of the remaining butter, the confectioners' sugar, cream and peppermint extract until thick and smooth. Spread evenly over the cake in the pan.
7. Melt the remaining ounce of chocolate and the remaining tablespoon of butter in the double boiler or heavy pan and pour it carefully over the mint frosting. Cool or refrigerate until the chocolate glaze is shiny. Remove from the pan and cut into bars. These brownies may be placed in the freezer and served frozen, if desired.

Spectator Brownies

Brown and white, like those shoes your mother wore with "sports clothes." You won't find many willing to be merely spectators with these goodies around, however.

Chocolate Layer:

5 OUNCES SEMISWEET CHOCOLATE
$\frac{1}{4}$ CUP UNSALTED BUTTER
2 LARGE EGGS
$\frac{1}{2}$ CUP SUGAR
$\frac{1}{2}$ CUP ALL-PURPOSE FLOUR
$\frac{1}{4}$ TEASPOON BAKING SODA
$\frac{1}{4}$ TEASPOON SALT

Cream Cheese Layer:

6 OUNCES CREAM CHEESE, AT ROOM
TEMPERATURE
2 TABLESPOONS BUTTER, AT ROOM
TEMPERATURE
I LARGE EGG
I TEASPOON VANILLA EXTRACT
$\frac{1}{2}$ CUP SUGAR
I TABLESPOON FLOUR

1. Preheat the oven to 350°F.
2. Butter and flour a 9-inch square baking pan.

3. For the chocolate layer, melt the chocolate and butter together in a double boiler over hot water or in a heavy pan over low heat. Cool.
4. In a large mixing bowl, beat the eggs and sugar together until thick and creamy. Beat in the chocolate mixture. Sift together the flour, baking soda and salt and stir them into the chocolate batter. Divide the batter in half and spread half over the bottom of the prepared pan.
5. For the cream cheese layer, cream the cheese and butter together and beat in the egg, vanilla and sugar. Stir in the flour until thoroughly incorporated.
6. Spread this mixture over the chocolate layer in the pan, then top with the remaining chocolate batter. If desired, insert a sharp knife through all the layers and make zigzag patterns to create a marbleized effect. Bake for about 35 minutes, until firm on top and/or a cake tester comes out almost clean.

Coconut Brownies

Crunchy and rich, these are slightly unorthodox in texture and taste.

3 OUNCES UNSWEETENED CHOCOLATE
1/2 CUP UNSALTED BUTTER
2 LARGE EGGS
I CUP SUGAR
I TEASPOON VANILLA EXTRACT
3/4 CUP ALL-PURPOSE FLOUR
1/2 TEASPOON BAKING POWDER
1/4 TEASPOON SALT
3/4 CUP SHREDDED COCONUT (FOUND IN MOST SUPERMARKETS)

1. Preheat the oven to 350°F.
2. Butter an 8-inch square baking pan.
3. Melt the chocolate and butter in a double boiler over hot water or in a heavy pan over low heat. Cool.
4. In a large mixing bowl, beat the eggs until lemon-colored and frothy. Beat in the sugar. Add the chocolate mixture and vanilla, mixing well. Sift the flour, baking powder and salt together and stir into the chocolate mixture. Stir in the coconut, blending all ingredients thoroughly.

5. Spread evenly in the prepared pan and bake for about 25 minutes or until top is firm and/or a cake tester comes out almost clean. Cool and cut into squares.

Church Supper Brownies

Here's a party to make in the oven! This recipe makes over 300 brownies. If you're lucky you'll have access to an industrial-size mixer; otherwise you may have to mix them laboriously by hand in a huge container. And if you're relying on home equipment, remember to allow enough time to bake them in six batches, unless you're lucky enough to have plenty of pans and an oven big enough for the whole job!

2½ POUNDS UNSALTED BUTTER
5 POUNDS SUGAR
16 LARGE EGGS
1 POUND UNSWEETENED COCOA
3 POUNDS CAKE FLOUR
1 TABLESPOON SALT
3 POUNDS CHOPPED WALNUTS

1. Preheat oven to 400°F.
2. Butter six 12 × 18-inch baking pans.

3. In a very large mixing bowl, cream the butter and sugar until smooth. Beat in the eggs. In a separate large bowl mix the cocoa, flour and salt; beat into the egg mixture. Stir in the nuts.
4. Divide the dough into six parts and spread one portion in each of the pans. Bake for about 25 minutes, or until firm on top and a cake tester comes out almost clean. Or spread a sixth of the batter into one baking pan and bake as above; repeat five times until all the brownies are baked. Cool and cut into 2-inch squares. Each batch yields 54 brownies, for a total of 324.

No-Bake Brownies

The all-time record for this easy-to-make treat is 15 minutes of preparation time, 10 minutes (maximum) of consumption time. This is a good recipe for kids to try, though you will want to supervise them in

4 OUNCES UNSWEETENED CHOCOLATE
2 TABLESPOONS UNSALTED BUTTER
I LARGE EGG
2 TABLESPOONS HEAVY CREAM
I TEASPOON VANILLA EXTRACT
½ TEASPOON SALT
I POUND CONFECTIONERS' SUGAR, SIFTED
I CUP CHOPPED WALNUTS

melting the chocolate and butter. And it's a delicious way to end a meal on a hot summer's day when you can't face heating the oven.

1. Butter an 8-inch square pan.
2. Melt the chocolate and butter in a double boiler over hot water or in a heavy pan over low heat. Beat in egg. Raise heat to medium and cook 3 minutes, stirring constantly. Cool slightly.
3. In a large mixing bowl, beat together the cream, vanilla, salt and confectioners' sugar. Beat in the chocolate mixture and fold in the nuts.
4. Spread the batter in the prepared pan and cool for 30 minutes, or refrigerate if desired. Cut into squares.

Sumptuous Brownies

Spirited and sybaritic! Many of these brownies feature after-dinner liqueurs, which make them perfect accompaniments for postprandial coffee and espresso.

Grand Marnier Brownies

One of the most sumptuous tastes in the world is that of Grand Marnier, a popular liqueur with the flavors of orange, almond, brandy and heaven knows what other wonderful things.

6 OUNCES BITTERSWEET CHOCOLATE
¾ CUP BUTTER
4 LARGE EGGS
1½ CUPS SUGAR
½ CUP HEAVY CREAM
1 TABLESPOON GRAND MARNIER LIQUEUR
2 TEASPOONS GRATED ORANGE ZEST
¼ TEASPOON VANILLA EXTRACT
¾ CUP ALL-PURPOSE FLOUR
¼ TEASPOON SALT

1. Preheat the oven to 350°F.
2. Butter and flour a 9 × 13-inch baking pan.
3. Melt the chocolate and butter in a double boiler over hot water or in a heavy pan over low heat. Cool.
4. In a large mixing bowl, beat the eggs and sugar until light-colored and creamy. Beat in the cream, Grand Marnier, orange peel and vanilla. Beat in the chocolate mixture. Stir in the flour and salt until completely combined.
5. Spread batter evenly in the prepared pan and bake about 25 minutes, until the edges pull away from the pan and/or a cake tester comes out clean. Cool and cut into squares.

Grasshopper Brownies

*Better than Grasshopper
Pie because it has
chocolate in it!*

3 OUNCES UNSWEETENED CHOCOLATE
¾ CUP UNSALTED BUTTER
2 LARGE EGGS
¼ TEASPOON SALT
4 TABLESPOONS CRÈME DE MENTHE
1 CUP SUGAR
½ CUP ALL-PURPOSE FLOUR
2 OUNCES COARSELY CHOPPED WALNUTS
1 CUP SIFTED CONFECTIONERS' SUGAR
1 TABLESPOON HEAVY WHIPPING CREAM
½ TEASPOON PEPPERMINT EXTRACT

1. Preheat the oven to 350°F.
2. Butter an 8-inch square pan. Line with waxed paper and butter the paper.
3. Melt 2 ounces of the chocolate and ½ cup of the butter in a double boiler over hot water or in a heavy pan over low heat. Cool.
4. In a large mixing bowl, beat the eggs until frothy. Beat in the salt, crème de menthe and sugar. Beat in the chocolate mixture and blend thoroughly. Stir in the flour and, before it is completely incorporated, add the nuts. Blend.

5. Pour into the prepared pan and bake for 30 minutes, until top is firm and/or a cake tester comes out clean. Cool.
6. To prepare the frosting, in a small mixing bowl combine 3 tablespoons of the softened butter, the confectioners' sugar, cream and peppermint extract and beat until smooth. Spread evenly over the brownies in the pan. Cool thoroughly.
7. To prepare the glaze, melt the remaining ounce of chocolate and the remaining tablespoon of butter in the double boiler or heavy pan. When smooth, pour the hot glaze over the frosted cake. Tilt the cake to spread the glaze evenly. Chill or refrigerate until the glaze is shiny. Remove from pan and cut into squares.

Amaretto Brownies

A little like brandy, a little like anisette, amaretto is one of today's most popular liqueur flavors. You'll love it in this delicate, cakelike brownie.

4 OUNCES SEMISWEET CHOCOLATE
1/2 CUP UNSALTED BUTTER
I TEASPOON INSTANT ESPRESSO
2 LARGE EGGS
2/3 CUP FIRMLY PACKED LIGHT BROWN SUGAR
1/3 CUP PLUS I TABLESPOON
AMARETTO LIQUEUR
3/4 CUP ALL-PURPOSE FLOUR
1/8 TEASPOON SALT
1/2 CUP CHOPPED TOASTED ALMONDS

1. Preheat the oven to 350°F.
2. Butter and flour an 8-inch square baking pan.
3. Melt the chocolate and butter together in a double boiler over hot water or in a heavy pan over low heat. Stir in the espresso to dissolve. Cool.
4. In a large mixing bowl, beat the eggs and sugar together until smooth and creamy. Beat in the chocolate-espresso mixture and 1/3 cup amaretto. Stir in the flour and salt and, when almost incorporated, add the almonds. Stir just enough to blend.

5. Spread the batter in the prepared pan and bake about 35 minutes, until firm on top and/or a cake tester comes out almost clean.
6. As the brownies come out of the oven, brush them with the remaining tablespoon of amaretto. Cool and cut into squares.

Bourbon Brownies

A family favorite. Even those who claim they don't like whiskey (bourbon is a type of whiskey) rave over this one.

2 TABLESPOONS RAISINS
1/4 CUP BOURBON
4 OUNCES BITTERSWEET CHOCOLATE
1/2 CUP UNSALTED BUTTER
2 LARGE EGGS
3/4 CUP SUGAR
1/3 CUP GROUND ALMONDS
1/2 CUP ALL-PURPOSE FLOUR
1/8 TEASPOON SALT

1. Preheat the oven to 350°F.
2. Butter and flour an 8-inch square baking pan.
3. Soak the raisins in the bourbon.
4. Melt the chocolate and butter in a double boiler over hot water or in a heavy pan over low heat. Cool.

5. In a large mixing bowl, beat together the eggs and sugar until light-colored and creamy. Beat in the chocolate mixture. Stir in the almonds, flour and salt until thoroughly combined. Stir in the raisins and bourbon.
6. Spread evenly in the prepared pan and bake about 30 minutes, until firm on top and/or a cake tester comes out nearly clean. Cool and cut into squares.

Brandied Brownies

The perfect after-dinner treat, with an elegant brandy-butter frosting on top.

5 OUNCES SEMISWEET CHOCOLATE
I CUP UNSALTED BUTTER AT ROOM TEMPERATURE, DIVIDED
3 LARGE EGGS PLUS I LARGE EGG YOLK
¾ CUP FIRMLY PACKED DARK BROWN SUGAR
6 TABLESPOONS COGNAC, ARMAGNAC, OR OTHER BRANDY, DIVIDED
I CUP ALL-PURPOSE FLOUR
¼ TEASPOON BAKING POWDER
¼ TEASPOON SALT
I ½ CUPS CHOPPED PECANS
½ CUP SUGAR
2 TABLESPOONS WATER

1. Preheat the oven to 350°F.
2. Butter a 9-inch square baking pan and line it with waxed paper. Butter the waxed paper and flour the entire pan.
3. Melt the chocolate and ½ cup of the butter in a double boiler over hot water or in a heavy pan over low heat. Cool.
4. In a large mixing bowl, beat the 3 eggs until lemon-colored and frothy. Beat in the brown sugar until smooth and creamy. Beat in the chocolate mixture and 3 tablespoons of the brandy.
5. Sift together the flour, baking powder and salt. Fold the flour mixture into the chocolate batter and, when almost incorporated, add the pecans.
6. Spread the batter evenly in the prepared pan and bake about 30 minutes, until the top is firm and/or a cake tester comes out nearly clean. Cool.
7. For the frosting, beat the egg yolk in a mixing bowl until thick and lemon-colored. Combine the water and the remaining 3 tablespoons of brandy in a saucepan and bring to a boil. Pour the brandy mixture slowly over the egg yolk in the mixing bowl, beating well. Return the mixture to the saucepan and bring slowly to a boil, stirring constantly. Beat in the butter a tablespoon at a time until frosting is smooth. Spread frosting over the brownies. Continue to cool. Cut into squares and remove to a serving plate.

Cheesecake Brownies

A quick and easy version of that New York favorite — cheesecake.

4 OUNCES SWEET CHOCOLATE
1 TEASPOON WATER
3 LARGE EGGS
6 OUNCES CREAM CHEESE, AT
ROOM TEMPERATURE
1 CUP SUGAR
1 CUP ALL-PURPOSE FLOUR
1/2 TEASPOON BAKING POWDER
1/4 TEASPOON SALT
1 TEASPOON VANILLA EXTRACT
1 TEASPOON GRATED LEMON ZEST

1. Preheat the oven to 350°F.
2. Butter and flour an 8-inch square baking pan.
3. Melt the chocolate with the water in a double boiler over hot water or in a heavy pan over low heat. Cool.
4. In a large mixing bowl, beat the eggs until lemon-colored and fluffy. Beat in the cream cheese until just combined. Beat in the sugar.
5. In a separate bowl, combine the flour, baking powder and salt,

then stir the flour mixture into the cream-cheese mixture along with the vanilla and the lemon zest. Set aside ½ cup of this batter.

6. Add the chocolate to the remainder of the batter, then spread half the chocolate batter in the prepared pan. Top with the reserved ½ cup of cream-cheese batter, dropping it in by spoonfuls and carefully spreading the spoonfuls out with a spatula to form an even layer. Add the remaining chocolate batter, spreading it evenly on top of the cream-cheese layer. Bake for about 30 minutes, until firm on top and/or a cake tester comes out nearly clean. Cool and cut into squares.

Triple Chocolate Pâté

Not quite a brownie, this is possibly the chocolate lover's dream come true. Serve it garnished with fresh strawberries and grapes to accent the chocolate's richness.

2 OUNCES UNSWEETENED CHOCOLATE
4 TABLESPOONS UNSALTED BUTTER
½ CUP SUGAR
¼ TEASPOON VANILLA EXTRACT
6 OUNCES WHITE CHOCOLATE
3 TABLESPOONS HEAVY CREAM
4 OUNCES SEMISWEET CHOCOLATE

1. Butter a 6- or 7-inch round, straight-sided pan or dish.
2. Melt the unsweetened chocolate with 2 tablespoons butter in a double boiler over hot water or in a heavy pan over low heat. Beat in the sugar until dissolved and the mixture is thick and smooth; beat in the vanilla.
3. Spread evenly over the bottom of the prepared pan. Cool or refrigerate until firm, about 30 to 45 minutes.
4. Melt the white chocolate with the cream in the (cleaned) double boiler or heavy pan, stirring very often to avoid discoloration. Spread evenly over the cooled unsweetened-chocolate mixture. Cool again until firm, about 30 to 45 minutes.
5. Melt the semisweet chocolate with the remaining 2 tablespoons butter in the (cleaned) double boiler or heavy pan and spread evenly over the cooled white chocolate mixture. Chill to set thoroughly.
6. Cut carefully into sliver-size pie slices and remove them from the pan.

Brownie Torte

Is it possible to improve upon a brownie? Here's proof.

6 OUNCES GROUND ALMONDS
1¼ CUPS SUGAR, DIVIDED
2 LARGE EGGS AND 1 LARGE EGG WHITE
3 OUNCES UNSWEETENED CHOCOLATE
½ CUP PLUS 1 TABLESPOON
UNSALTED BUTTER
1 TEASPOON VANILLA EXTRACT
½ CUP ALL-PURPOSE FLOUR
¼ TEASPOON SALT
¼ CUP RASPBERRY JAM, PREFERABLY SEEDLESS

1. Combine the almonds with ¼ cup of the sugar. Beat the egg white separately until frothy, then add it to the almond mixture. Soften 1 tablespoon of the butter and blend it into the mixture. Form into a ball, wrap in plastic wrap and chill for 1 hour (or overnight).
2. Preheat the oven to 350°F.
3. Butter a 9-inch square pan.
4. Roll out refrigerated mixture on a floured bread board into a 9-inch square and fit it into the prepared pan. Cover with buttered foil and bake for 20 minutes. Remove the foil and let cool in the pan.
5. Melt the chocolate and ½ cup butter in a double boiler over hot

water or in a heavy pan over low heat. In a large mixing bowl, beat the eggs until lemon-colored and frothy, then add the remaining 1 cup sugar gradually, beating well. Beat the mixture well until light-colored and thick. Stir in the chocolate mixture and the vanilla. Stir in the flour and salt.

6. Spread the jam evenly over the almond crust in the pan.
7. Top with brownie batter, spreading it evenly. Bake for about 25 minutes, or until a cake tester comes out with crumbs. Cool thoroughly before removing from the pan.

Blondies

These light-colored squares may or may not have chocolate in them. They can achieve their golden effect with a brown-sugar/butter combination, with butterscotch or with white chocolate. What matters is that they're easy to make and absolutely delicious.

The Traditional Blondie

Chewy with just bits of chocolate, these toasty-brown blondies are Dagwood's favorite.

½ CUP BUTTER
I CUP FIRMLY PACKED LIGHT BROWN SUGAR
I LARGE EGG
I TEASPOON VANILLA EXTRACT
I CUP ALL-PURPOSE FLOUR
½ TEASPOON SALT
6 OUNCES SEMISWEET CHOCOLATE BITS

1. Preheat the oven to 350°F.
2. Butter an 8-inch square baking pan.
3. Melt the butter in a small heavy pan over low heat. Stir in the sugar until smooth and dissolved. Transfer the mixture to a large mixing bowl and beat 1 minute. Add the egg and vanilla and beat until light and fluffy, scraping down the sides of the bowl occasionally. Stir in the flour and salt until just blended. Fold in the chocolate bits.
4. Spread evenly in the prepared pan and bake about 25 to 30 minutes, until firm on top and/or a cake tester comes out clean. Do not overbake. Cool and cut into squares.

Butterscotch Blondies

Are they blondies if they don't have any chocolate in them? While the experts struggle with this thorny question, we'll enjoy the following irresistible recipe.

12 OUNCES BUTTERSCOTCH BITS
½ CUP BUTTER
1½ CUPS FIRMLY PACKED LIGHT BROWN SUGAR
1½ CUPS ALL-PURPOSE FLOUR
1 TEASPOON BAKING POWDER
1 TEASPOON SALT
3 LARGE EGGS
1 TEASPOON VANILLA EXTRACT
½ CUP CHOPPED UNSALTED CASHEWS

1. Preheat the oven to 350°F.
2. Butter a 9-inch square baking pan.
3. Melt the butterscotch bits and butter together in a double boiler over hot water or in a heavy pan over a low flame. Transfer the mixture to a large mixing bowl and beat in the brown sugar until smooth and dissolved. Cool.
4. Sift together the flour, baking powder and salt.
5. Beat the eggs and vanilla into the butterscotch mixture. Gradually add the flour mixture. When almost incorporated, add the nuts.
6. Spread evenly in the prepared pan and bake for 30 minutes, or until firm on top and/or a cake tester comes out almost clean. Cool and cut into squares.

Butterscotch Molasses Brownies

These aren't chocolate either, but they're deep, dark and delicious.

½ CUP UNSALTED BUTTER
¼ CUP MOLASSES
1 TEASPOON VANILLA EXTRACT
1 CUP FIRMLY PACKED DARK BROWN SUGAR
2 LARGE EGGS
1 CUP ALL-PURPOSE FLOUR
½ CUP CHOPPED WALNUTS

1. Preheat the oven to 350°F.
2. Butter a 9-inch baking pan.
3. In a heavy pan melt the butter. Add the molasses and stir well to combine. Cool. Transfer the mixture to a large mixing bowl and beat in the vanilla and brown sugar. Add the eggs one at a time, beating well after each addition. Beat for a few minutes, scraping down the bowl as necessary, until the mixture is smooth and light-colored. Blend in the flour and when almost incorporated, stir in the nuts.
4. Spread evenly in the prepared pan and bake about 30 minutes, or until firm on top and/or a cake tester comes out almost clean. Cool and cut into squares.

Butterscotch Brownies

At last, butterscotch brownies with chocolate in them! (Well, in the frosting, anyway.)

½ CUP UNSALTED BUTTER
I CUP FIRMLY PACKED LIGHT BROWN SUGAR
I LARGE EGG
½ TEASPOON VANILLA EXTRACT
2 TABLESPOONS RUM
I CUP ALL-PURPOSE FLOUR
½ TEASPOON BAKING POWDER
½ TEASPOON SALT
½ CUP CHOPPED PECANS
2 OUNCES SEMISWEET CHOCOLATE

1. Preheat the oven to 350°F.
2. Butter an 8-inch square baking pan.
3. Melt 6 tablespoons of the butter in a heavy pan. Combine with the brown sugar and blend thoroughly. Cool slightly. Beat in the egg, vanilla and rum.
4. Sift together the flour, baking powder and salt and stir it into the butterscotch mixture. Stir in the nuts. Spread evenly in the prepared pan and bake for 20 minutes, until the top is firm and/or a cake tester comes out clean. Cool.
5. Melt the remaining 2 tablespoons of butter with the chocolate in a

double boiler over hot water or in a heavy pan over low heat. Cool slightly. Pour the frosting over the brownies and tilt the pan back and forth so the brownies are evenly covered. Cool until the frosting is firm and shiny. Cut into squares.

Peanut Butter Blondies

Crunchy, crumbly and scrumptious. And ah, the aroma!

$^1/_3$ CUP CHUNKY PEANUT BUTTER
$^1/_4$ CUP UNSALTED BUTTER AT ROOM TEMPERATURE
$^3/_4$ CUP FIRMLY PACKED LIGHT BROWN SUGAR
$^3/_4$ CUP SUGAR
2 LARGE EGGS
1 TEASPOON VANILLA EXTRACT
1 $^1/_3$ CUPS ALL-PURPOSE FLOUR
$^1/_2$ CUP UNSWEETENED COCOA
1 TEASPOON BAKING POWDER
$^1/_2$ TEASPOON SALT
$^3/_4$ CUP SALTED PEANUTS, CHOPPED

1. Preheat the oven to 350°F.
2. Butter and flour a 9-inch baking pan.
3. In a large mixing bowl, beat the peanut butter and butter together until creamy and smooth (except for the peanut chunks). Beat in the sugars until smooth. Beat in the eggs one at a time, beating well after each addition. Blend in the vanilla.
4. Combine the flour, cocoa, baking powder and salt in a separate mixing bowl, then beat the dry ingredients into the peanut butter mixture until thoroughly incorporated.
5. Scrape the mixture into the prepared pan and spread evenly. Sprinkle the nuts over the top and lightly press them in. Bake for about 30 minutes, until firm on top and/or a cake tester comes out clean. Cool and cut into squares.

Tropical Blondies

*A pirate's treasure — a
taste of the tropics in a
white chocolate blondie.*

6 OUNCES WHITE CHOCOLATE, DIVIDED
1/2 CUP UNSALTED BUTTER
3 LARGE EGGS
1 1/2 CUPS SUGAR
1 TEASPOON VANILLA EXTRACT
1 1/2 CUPS ALL-PURPOSE FLOUR
1/4 TEASPOON SALT
1/2 CUP CHOPPED TOASTED MACADAMIA
NUTS, PREFERABLY UNSALTED
1/2 CUP CHOPPED DRIED PINEAPPLE
1 CUP SHREDDED COCONUT

1. Preheat the oven to 350°F.
2. Butter and flour a 9 × 13-inch baking pan.
3. Melt 3 ounces of the chocolate and the butter in a double boiler over hot water or in a heavy pan over low heat. Cool.
4. In a large mixing bowl, beat the eggs until lemon-colored and frothy, then beat in the sugar until smooth and creamy. Beat in the chocolate mixture and vanilla. Stir in the flour and salt until almost incorporated, then stir in the nuts and pineapple.

5. Spread the batter evenly in the prepared pan and bake for about 35 minutes, until firm on top and a cake tester comes out clean. Cool.
6. While the blondies are baking, melt the remaining 3 ounces of white chocolate in a double boiler or heavy pan. Stir in the coconut. Spread over the cooled blondies and let the frosting cool as well. Cut into squares.

Caramel Brownies

These are made with dark chocolate but covered with a caramel icing — brownie inside, blondie outside.

¾ CUP UNSALTED BUTTER AT ROOM TEMPERATURE, DIVIDED
1 CUP SUGAR
2 LARGE EGGS
1 ½ TEASPOONS VANILLA EXTRACT, DIVIDED
¼ CUP UNSWEETENED COCOA
½ CUP ALL-PURPOSE FLOUR
1 CUP CHOPPED PECANS
1 ½ CUPS FIRMLY PACKED LIGHT BROWN SUGAR
½ CUP HEAVY CREAM

1. Preheat the oven to 350°F.
2. Butter an 8-inch square baking pan.
3. In a large mixing bowl, cream ½ cup of the butter and the sugar together. Beat in the eggs one at a time, beating well after each addition. Blend in 1 teaspoon of the vanilla.
4. In a small bowl stir together the cocoa and flour with a fork until combined. Stir the cocoa mixture into the batter and add the nuts.
5. Spread evenly in the prepared pan and bake for about 30 minutes, until firm on top and/or a cake tester comes out nearly clean. Cool.
6. To make the caramel frosting, cook the brown sugar and cream, stirring, until the sugar dissolves. Continue to cook, bubbling, until a drop of the syrup forms a soft ball when dropped into cold water (234°F. on a candy thermometer). Remove from the heat and add the remaining ¼ cup butter. Let cool slightly, then beat in the butter and the remaining ½ teaspoon vanilla until the frosting is creamy. Spread immediately on the brownies.

Healthy Brownies

Just because they taste decadent doesn't mean brownies can't be good for you. These are recipes you'll feel good about serving to your children. Actually, you can make any brownie more nutritious by using whole-grain flours, substituting polyunsaturated vegetable oils for some of the butter, and adding toasted sunflower or pumpkin seeds.

Granola Brownies

A nutritious treat with a hearty, homey flavor . . . and the comforting feeling that you're eating well. Serve these to the kids with no guilt.

½ CUP VEGETABLE OIL (PREFERABLY UNHYDROGENATED)
1½ CUPS FIRMLY PACKED LIGHT BROWN SUGAR
2 LARGE EGGS
1 TEASPOON VANILLA EXTRACT
¾ CUPS UNBLEACHED WHITE FLOUR (FOUND IN HEALTH-FOOD STORES)
¾ CUP WHOLE-WHEAT FLOUR
1 TEASPOON BAKING SODA
1 TEASPOON SALT
1 TEASPOON CINNAMON
1½ CUPS GRANOLA (PLAIN, WITH MINIMUM SWEETENERS AND FAT ADDED)
½ CUP CHOPPED WALNUTS
½ CUP UNSULFURED RAISINS

1. Preheat the oven to 350°F.
2. Butter a 9 × 13-inch baking pan.
3. In a large mixing bowl, beat the oil and sugar together until smooth. Beat in the eggs and vanilla.
4. In a separate bowl, stir together the flours, baking soda, salt and

cinnamon. Blend the flour mixture into the oil-sugar mixture thoroughly. Stir in the granola, nuts and raisins.

5. Spread the batter evenly in the prepared pan. Bake for 25 minutes, until firm on top and/or a cake tester comes out clean. Cool and cut into squares.

Variation: For a hint of naughtiness add ½ cup semisweet chocolate bits (or carob bits) along with the nuts and raisins.

Honey Brownies

Light and fresh . . . a gift from the bees. The honey keeps these brownies fresh, moist and tasty for days.

4 OUNCES UNSWEETENED CHOCOLATE
1/2 CUP UNSALTED BUTTER
3/4 CUP HONEY, PREFERABLY UNFILTERED
3 LARGE EGGS
3/4 CUP SUGAR
1 CUP UNBLEACHED WHITE FLOUR
1/2 CUP CHOPPED ALMONDS

1. Preheat the oven to 325°F.
2. Butter a 9-inch square baking pan and line it with waxed paper. Butter the waxed paper, then flour the entire pan.
3. Melt the chocolate and butter in a double boiler over hot water or in a heavy pan over low heat. Stir in the honey until softened and blended; let cool.
4. In a large mixing bowl, beat the eggs until lemon-colored and frothy, then add the sugar and beat until thick and creamy. Beat in the chocolate mixture until completely incorporated. Stir in the flour, then the nuts.
5. Spread the batter evenly in the prepared pan and bake about 35 minutes, until firm on top and/or a cake tester comes out clean. Cool and cut into squares.

Graham Cracker Brownies

Graham flour contains a higher percentage of natural wheat fiber than bleached white flour (though less than whole-grain flours). These healthful brownies will please kids of all ages.

3 LARGE EGGS
1/4 CUP HEAVY CREAM
1/2 CUP SUGAR
1 CUP FIRMLY PACKED LIGHT BROWN SUGAR
1 TEASPOON VANILLA EXTRACT
1/2 TEASPOON SALT
2 1/2 CUP GRAHAM CRACKER CRUMBS
(ABOUT 30 SQUARES, CRUMBLED)
3/4 CUP CHOPPED WALNUTS

1. Preheat the oven to 350°F.
2. Butter and flour a 9 × 13-inch baking pan.
3. In a large mixing bowl, beat the eggs until lemon-colored and frothy. Beat in the cream, the sugars, the vanilla and the salt, and beat until thick and smooth. Stir in the graham cracker crumbs until thoroughly blended, then stir in the nuts.
4. Spread the batter evenly in the prepared baking pan and bake for about 20 minutes, until firm on top and/or a cake tester comes out clean. Cool and cut into squares.

Apple Raisin Brownies

These spicy, aromatic cakes sport a zesty orange glaze.

1 OUNCE UNSWEETENED CHOCOLATE
6 TABLESPOONS UNSALTED BUTTER
1 CUP FIRMLY PACKED LIGHT BROWN SUGAR
½ CUP SUGAR
½ CUP UNSWEETENED APPLESAUCE
1 LARGE EGG
1 TEASPOON VANILLA
1 ½ CUPS ALL-PURPOSE FLOUR
1 TEASPOON BAKING POWDER
½ TEASPOON SALT
½ TEASPOON CINNAMON
¼ TEASPOON ALLSPICE
½ CUP UNSULFURED RAISINS
½ CUP CHOPPED WALNUTS
½ CUP CONFECTIONERS' SUGAR
1 TABLESPOON FROZEN ORANGE JUICE
CONCENTRATE, THAWED

1. Preheat the oven to 350°F.
2. Butter and flour a 9 × 13-inch baking pan.
3. Melt the chocolate and butter in a double boiler over hot water or

in a heavy pan over low heat. Cool, then transfer to a large mixing bowl.

4. Beat the sugars, applesauce, egg and vanilla into the chocolate. In a separate bowl, stir together the flour, baking powder, salt, cinnamon and allspice. Add the applesauce mixture and blend well. Stir in the raisins and nuts.

5. Spread the batter evenly in the prepared pan and bake for 25 minutes, until firm on top and/or a cake tester comes out clean. Cool slightly.

6. To prepare the glaze, sift the confectioners' sugar into a bowl and stir in the thawed orange juice concentrate until smooth. Spread over the brownies while they are still warm. Cool until the glaze sets. Cut into squares.

Trail Mix Brownies

So easy, you can make them over the campfire. Experiment with your favorite trail mix — gorp ("good old raisins and peanuts") or fancier varieties with coconut, tropical fruits, pumpkin seeds, etc.

4 OUNCES UNSWEETENED CHOCOLATE
I CUP UNSALTED BUTTER
EGG SUBSTITUTE EQUIVALENT OF I LARGE EGG (AVAILABLE IN MANY CAMPING STORES), OPTIONAL (BROWNIES WILL BE VERY FUDGELIKE IF EGG IS OMITTED)
2 TABLESPOONS EVAPORATED MILK
I TEASPOON VANILLA EXTRACT
½ TEASPOON SALT
I CUP CONFECTIONERS' SUGAR
I CUP TRAIL MIX

1. Butter an 8-inch square pan.
2. Melt the chocolate and butter in a double boiler over hot water or in a heavy pan over low heat. (If you're camping, place the chocolate and butter in a covered heat-proof container in the ashes near the campfire. Stir the mixture frequently.) Let cool.
3. In a large mixing bowl beat together the egg substitute (if used), milk, vanilla extract, and salt until smooth, then beat in the sugar. (If using powdered egg substitute, reconstitute according to package directions.) Stir in the chocolate mixture. Fold in the trail mix and spread the batter in the prepared pan. Let cool completely and cut into squares.

Breakfast Brownies

A cakelike brownie, with a wake-up morning flavor combination of coffee and oatmeal. Who says you can't have brownies for breakfast?

8 OUNCES SEMISWEET CHOCOLATE
1/2 CUP UNSALTED BUTTER
1 TABLESPOON POWDERED INSTANT COFFEE
2 LARGE EGGS
1 1/2 CUPS FIRMLY PACKED LIGHT BROWN SUGAR
1 1/2 CUPS ALL-PURPOSE FLOUR
1 TEASPOON BAKING POWDER
1/2 TEASPOON SALT
1 CUP OLD-FASHIONED ROLLED OATS
1/4 CUP CHOPPED ALMONDS

1. Preheat the oven to 375°F.
2. Butter and flour a 9 × 13-inch baking pan.
3. Melt the chocolate and butter in a double boiler over hot water or in a heavy pan over low heat. Stir in the instant coffee, then cool.
4. In a large mixing bowl, beat the eggs until lemon-colored and foamy. Beat in the sugar until thick and smooth. Beat in the chocolate mixture. Sift together the flour, baking powder and salt and stir the flour mixture along with the oatmeal into the chocolate batter. When almost completely incorporated, stir in the nuts.

5. Spread the batter evenly in the prepared pan and bake for about 30 minutes, until firm on top and/or a cake tester comes out almost clean. Cool and cut into squares.

Maple-Glazed Carrot Brownies

Just as maple syrup makes a delicious glaze for steamed carrots, it tops these carrot brownies with sweet panache.

4 OUNCES UNSWEETENED CHOCOLATE
1/2 CUP UNSALTED BUTTER
2 LARGE EGGS
1/2 CUP SUGAR
1/2 CUP FIRMLY PACKED LIGHT BROWN SUGAR
I TEASPOON VANILLA EXTRACT
I CUP UNBLEACHED WHITE FLOUR
I TEASPOON BAKING POWDER
1/2 TEASPOON SALT
1/2 TEASPOON GROUND GINGER
I CUP SHREDDED CARROTS (ABOUT I OR 2 CARROTS)
1/2 CUP RAISINS
1/2 CUP PURE MAPLE SYRUP
I TABLESPOON CORN SYRUP

1. Preheat the oven to 350°F.
2. Butter a 9-inch square baking pan.
3. Melt the chocolate and butter in a double boiler over hot water or in a heavy pan over low heat. Cool.
4. In a large mixing bowl, beat the eggs lightly, then beat in the sugars, the chocolate mixture, and the vanilla.
5. In a separate bowl stir together the flour, baking powder, salt and ginger. Stir the flour mixture and the carrots into the batter, then stir in the raisins.
6. Spread the batter in the prepared pan and bake for about 35 minutes, until firm on top and/or a cake tester comes out clean. Let cool.
7. In a small heavy saucepan combine the maple and corn syrups and bring to a boil over high heat. Swirl the pan by the handle to keep the contents from sticking. Lower the heat and continue cooking and swirling until the syrup is a rich brown caramel color. Remove from the heat and pour slowly over the brownies, then tilt the pan to distribute the glaze evenly. Cool until the glaze is set. Cut into squares.

Healthy Heart Brownies

It's not the chocolate in brownies that makes your cholesterol soar, it's the cocoa fat and the butter. (Unsweetened cocoa has less fat than bar chocolates, but carob powder has even less than cocoa.) So here's a version that cuts those LDLs down to size. Not for everyday consumption by heart patients, but a special treat.

I CUP UNBLEACHED WHITE FLOUR
I TEASPOON BAKING POWDER
1/2 CUP CANOLA OIL (SEE NOTE)
1/2 CUP UNSWEETENED COCOA OR CAROB POWDER
I CUP SUGAR
I TEASPOON VANILLA EXTRACT
1/2 TEASPOON GRATED LEMON ZEST
3 EGG WHITES
1/2 CUP RAISINS

1. Preheat the oven to 350°F.
2. Oil a 9-inch square baking pan.
3. Stir together the flour and baking powder, and set aside. In a separate large mixing bowl, beat the oil and cocoa or carob powder until thick and smooth. Beat in the sugar, vanilla and lemon zest

until smooth. Add the egg whites one at a time, beating well after each addition. Stir in the flour mixture until almost incorporated; then stir in the raisins.

4. Spread evenly in the prepared pan and bake for about 35 minutes, until firm on top and/or a cake tester comes out nearly clean. Cool and cut into squares.

Note: Canola oil, or Canada oil, is made from rapeseed grown in Canada and northern Europe. It is the cholesterol watcher's best choice of dietary fat, lower in saturated fat than any other vegetable oil, high in the valuable polyunsaturates and highest in monounsaturates (as is olive oil).

International Brownies

Wherever desserts are served, chocolate is cherished. Bakers around the world have been creating all forms of chocolate treats or their equivalents for centuries. The language of brownies is international.

Black Forest Brownies

Built upon a cake with a
fudgy interior, these
brownies also have a
cherry-hazelnut filling
and a deep, dark
chocolate frosting.

½ CUP UNSALTED BUTTER
¾ CUP FIRMLY PACKED DARK BROWN
SUGAR, DIVIDED
1 CUP ALL-PURPOSE FLOUR
½ TEASPOON SALT, DIVIDED
2 LARGE EGGS
½ TEASPOON VANILLA EXTRACT
2 TABLESPOONS KIRSCH OR CHERRY BRANDY
2 TABLESPOONS UNSWEETENED COCOA
1 CUP GROUND HAZELNUTS OR ALMONDS
½ CUP CHERRY PRESERVES
4 OUNCES SEMISWEET CHOCOLATE
2 TABLESPOONS CONFECTIONERS' SUGAR
2 TEASPOONS STRONG PREPARED COFFEE
2 TEASPOONS BOILING WATER

1. Preheat the oven to 375°F.
2. Lightly butter and flour a 9-inch square baking pan.
3. In a large mixing bowl, cream the butter and ¼ cup brown sugar
   until thick and smooth. Add flour and ¼ teaspoon of the salt and
   beat only until blended. Spread evenly in the prepared pan and
   bake for 10 minutes.

4. While the first layer is baking, beat the eggs in a large mixing bowl until slightly thickened. Add the vanilla, the kirsch and the remaining salt, and blend in the remaining brown sugar and cocoa. Beat a few minutes to blend thoroughly. Mix in the ground hazelnuts.
5. Stir the cherry preserves and spread them evenly over the hot cake to within ½ inch of the edges.
6. Pour the filling over the preserves, tilting the pan back and forth to distribute it evenly. Bake for 25 minutes; cool.
7. Melt the semisweet chocolate in a double boiler over hot water or in a heavy pan over low heat. Stir in the sugar, coffee and boiling water until smooth. Spread the frosting evenly over the cake. Cool and cut into squares. Serve *mit Schlag* (with whipped cream) if desired. You may wish to garnish these brownies with chocolate-dipped cherries.

Greek Truffles

A traditional favorite with chocolate lovers throughout the culinary wonderland of Greece. No cooking required!

8 OUNCES MILK CHOCOLATE
1 CUP GROUND WALNUTS
1/2 CUP GROUND HAZELNUTS
1/4 CUP GROUND ALMONDS
1/2 CUP CONFECTIONERS' SUGAR
1 TABLESPOON HEAVY CREAM AT ROOM TEMPERATURE
1 TABLESPOON BRANDY
1/4 CUP UNSWEETENED COCOA
BLANCHED ALMONDS (ABOUT 36)

1. Melt the chocolate in a large bowl over hot water. Add all the nuts, the sugar, the cream and the brandy. If the mixture is too stiff, add a little more cream. Let mixture cool.
2. Shape the mixture into balls by tablespoonfuls, rolling them between your palms. Roll each ball in the cocoa and top it with a blanched almond.

   Makes about 3 dozen truffles.

Double Dutch Brownies

One layer is crispy and crunchy, the other thick and moist. The Dutch seem to like things in two parts (Dutch doors or Double Dutch rope-jumping). These brownies can be made without an electric mixer.

1 CUP ALL-PURPOSE FLOUR, DIVIDED
1/2 TEASPOON BAKING SODA, DIVIDED
1/2 TEASPOON SALT, DIVIDED
1/2 CUP FIRMLY PACKED LIGHT BROWN SUGAR
1 CUP OLD-FASHIONED ROLLED OATS
1/2 CUP FINELY CHOPPED WALNUTS
12 TABLESPOONS UNSALTED BUTTER, DIVIDED
2 OUNCES UNSWEETENED CHOCOLATE
1 CUP SUGAR
1 EGG
1 TEASPOON VANILLA EXTRACT

1. Preheat the oven to 350°F.
2. Lightly butter an 8-inch square baking pan.
3. Sift together 1/3 cup of the flour, 1/4 teaspoon of the baking soda and 1/4 teaspoon of the salt in a large mixing bowl. Stir in the brown sugar and mix thoroughly. Stir in the oatmeal and nuts, then work in 6 tablespoons of the butter, cut into little pieces, until the mixture is well blended but crumbly.
4. Press evenly into the prepared pan and bake for 15 minutes.

5. Melt the chocolate and the remaining 6 tablespoons of butter in a double boiler over hot water or in a heavy pan over low heat. Cool.
6. Mix the sugar into the chocolate, then add the egg, stirring until well mixed. Stir in the vanilla. Sift together the remaining ⅔ cup of flour, ¼ teaspoon of baking soda and ¼ teaspoon of salt; add this mixture to the chocolate batter and blend until smooth.
7. Pour the mixture over the still-warm baked layer in the pan. Bake for about 30 minutes, until firm on top and/or a cake tester comes out almost clean. Cool and cut into squares.

Brownies du Barry

Louis the Fifteenth's favorite mistress would have loved these, culinary expert that she was.

4 OUNCES UNSWEETENED CHOCOLATE
½ CUP BUTTER
2 CUPS SUGAR, DIVIDED
2 EGGS, SEPARATED
2 TEASPOONS VANILLA EXTRACT
1½ CUPS ALL-PURPOSE FLOUR
2 TEASPOONS BAKING POWDER
½ TEASPOON SALT
1 CUP MILK

1. Preheat the oven to 350°F.
2. Butter a 9 × 13-inch baking pan. Line it with waxed paper, then butter the waxed paper. Flour the entire pan.
3. Melt the chocolate in a double boiler over hot water or in a heavy pan over low heat. Cool.
4. In a large mixing bowl, cream the butter. Add 1½ cups of the sugar and beat until light and fluffy. Add the egg yolks and the vanilla. Sift together the flour, baking powder and salt. Add to the batter alternately with the milk, beating after each addition.
5. Beat the egg whites until they form stiff peaks. Beat in the remaining ½ cup sugar. Fold carefully into the chocolate mixture.
6. Spread evenly in the prepared pan and bake about 40 minutes, until firm on top and/or a cake tester comes out almost clean.

Brazilian Brownies

There's an awful lot of coffee in Brazil, and Brazil nuts, too. Samba around the kitchen while you're preparing these, to work off the calories.

4 OUNCES UNSWEETENED CHOCOLATE
2 OUNCES SEMISWEET CHOCOLATE
3/4 CUP UNSALTED BUTTER
1 TABLESPOON POWDERED INSTANT COFFEE
3 EGGS
1 1/2 CUPS SUGAR
1 TABLESPOON GRATED ORANGE ZEST
1 TEASPOON VANILLA EXTRACT
3/4 CUP ALL-PURPOSE FLOUR
1/4 TEASPOON SALT
1/4 CUP CHOPPED BRAZIL NUTS

1. Preheat the oven to 350°F.
2. Butter an 8-inch square baking pan. Line the pan with waxed paper, then butter the paper. Flour the entire pan.
3. Melt the two kinds of chocolate and the butter in a double boiler over hot water or in a heavy pan over low heat. Stir in the coffee powder to dissolve. Cool.
4. In a large mixing bowl, beat the eggs until lemon-colored and frothy. Add the sugar and beat until thick and creamy. Beat in the orange zest and vanilla. Stir in the flour and salt. When almost incorporated, stir in the nuts.

5. Spread the batter evenly in the prepared pan and bake for about 35 minutes, until firm on top and/or a cake tester comes out nearly clean. Cool and cut into squares.

British Treacle Brownies

Treacle, or molasses, has always had an important place in British baking. This recipe makes a dense, dark brownie with the robust flavor of English stout to round out the chocolate.

¼ CUP RAISINS
¼ CUP STOUT
4 OUNCES UNSWEETENED CHOCOLATE
½ CUP UNSALTED BUTTER
⅓ CUP MOLASSES (NOT BLACKSTRAP)
¾ CUP FIRMLY PACKED DARK BROWN SUGAR
2 EGGS
¾ CUP ALL-PURPOSE FLOUR
¼ TEASPOON SALT
PINCH OF NUTMEG

1. Preheat the oven to 350°F.
2. Butter and flour an 8-inch square baking pan.
3. Soak the raisins in the stout.

4. Melt the chocolate and the butter in a double boiler over hot water or in a heavy pan over low heat. Stir in the molasses. Cool.
5. In a large mixing bowl, beat the sugar and the eggs together until thick and creamy. Blend in the chocolate-molasses mixture until thoroughly combined. Stir in the flour, salt and nutmeg. Stir in the stout and raisins until blended.
6. Pour the mixture into the prepared pan and bake about 35 to 40 minutes, until firm on top and/or a cake tester comes out nearly clean.

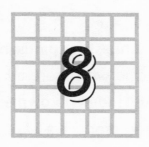

The Brownie Controversy: Fudgy versus Cakelike

Perhaps you've already decided whether you prefer your brownies light, delicate and crumbly like a fine cake, or dense and chewy like fudge. If not, here are some recipes for brownies on both sides of the fence to help you in your quest for partisanship.

In general, a recipe with more chocolate and butter and less flour makes fudgier brownies. Almost any recipe can be altered to produce a cakelike texture simply by using a slightly smaller pan than that indicated in the recipe (for instance, an 8-inch square pan in place of a 9-inch square one).

Chocolate Cake Brownies

Light and crumbly, this delicate treat is sure to please everyone.

½ CUP UNSALTED BUTTER AT ROOM TEMPERATURE

½ CUP FIRMLY PACKED LIGHT BROWN SUGAR

½ CUP SUGAR

2 LARGE EGGS

1 TEASPOON VANILLA EXTRACT

¾ CUP ALL-PURPOSE FLOUR

½ CUP UNSWEETENED COCOA

1 TEASPOON BAKING POWDER

¼ TEASPOON SALT

½ CUP CHOPPED WALNUTS

---

1. Preheat the oven to 350°F.
2. Butter and flour an 8-inch square baking pan.
3. In a large mixing bowl, cream the butter and sugars together until light-colored and fluffy. Beat in the eggs one at a time, beating well after each addition; beat in the vanilla. In a separate bowl, stir together the flour, cocoa, baking powder and salt until well combined, then stir the flour mixture into the butter-sugar mixture until just blended. Stir in the nuts.

4. Spread the batter evenly in the prepared pan and bake about 30 minutes, until firm on top and/or a cake tester comes out clean. Cool and cut into squares.

Coconut Brownies

This cakelike brownie achieves a special texture with ground almonds and shredded coconut. (If you can't find unsweetened coconut, you can use the sweetened variety and reduce the sugar to ¹/₂ cup.)

4 OUNCES BITTERSWEET CHOCOLATE
¹/₂ CUP MELTED BUTTER
2 LARGE EGGS
³/₄ CUP SUGAR
1 CUP FINELY GROUND ALMONDS
¹/₄ CUP ALL-PURPOSE FLOUR
1 CUP UNSWEETENED SHREDDED COCONUT
(AVAILABLE AT SOME HEALTH-FOOD STORES AND MIDDLE EASTERN SHOPS)
16 WHOLE BLANCHED ALMONDS

1. Preheat the oven to 350°F.
2. Butter an 8-inch square baking pan. Line the bottom with waxed paper, then butter the paper.
3. Melt the chocolate and butter in a double boiler over hot water or in a heavy pan over low heat. Cool.

4. In a large mixing bowl, beat the eggs until lemon-colored and frothy. Beat in the sugar until thick and smooth. Beat in the chocolate mixture.
5. In a separate bowl, blend the ground almonds and the flour until thoroughly combined, then beat into the batter. Stir in the coconut. Spread the batter evenly in the prepared pan and place the whole almonds in four rows of four, evenly spaced, on top of the batter. Press in lightly.
6. Bake about 20 minutes, until firm on top and/or a cake tester comes out clean. Cool and cut into 16 squares.

Fudge Brownies

This is your basic evil fudge brownie.

3 OUNCES UNSWEETENED CHOCOLATE
1/2 CUP UNSALTED BUTTER
2 LARGE EGGS
1 CUP SUGAR
1 TEASPOON VANILLA EXTRACT
2/3 CUP ALL-PURPOSE FLOUR
1/2 TEASPOON BAKING POWDER
1/4 TEASPOON SALT
1/2 CUP CHOPPED WALNUTS OR PECANS

1. Preheat the oven to 350°F.
2. Butter and flour an 8-inch square baking pan.
3. Melt the chocolate and the butter together in a double boiler over hot water or in a heavy pan over low heat. Cool.
4. In a large mixing bowl, beat the eggs until lemon-colored and frothy. Beat in the sugar until thick and smooth, then beat in the vanilla. Add the chocolate mixture and beat well. In a separate bowl, sift together the flour, baking powder and salt. Stir the flour mixture into the chocolate batter until almost incorporated, then stir in the nuts.
5. Spread evenly in the prepared pan and bake about 25 minutes, until firm on top and/or a cake tester comes out with crumbs. Cool and cut into squares.

Chewy Brownies

Moist and fudgy, these brownies will give you something to sink your teeth into.

4 OUNCES UNSWEETENED CHOCOLATE
1 CUP UNSALTED BUTTER
3 LARGE EGGS
1 CUP SUGAR
3/4 CUP FIRMLY PACKED LIGHT BROWN SUGAR
1 TEASPOON VANILLA EXTRACT
1 CUP ALL-PURPOSE FLOUR
1/4 TEASPOON SALT
1/2 CUP CHOPPED PECANS

1. Preheat the oven to 350°F.
2. Butter a 9-inch square baking pan. Line the bottom with waxed paper, then butter again. Flour the pan.
3. Melt the chocolate and butter in a double boiler over hot water or in a heavy pan over low heat. Cool.
4. In a large mixing bowl, beat the eggs until lemon-colored and frothy. Beat in the sugars until thick and smooth. Beat in the vanilla. Add the chocolate mixture and beat just to blend. Stir in the flour and salt until almost incorporated, then stir in the nuts.
5. Spread evenly in the prepared pan and bake for about 30 minutes, until firm on top and/or a cake tester comes out nearly clean. Cool and cut into squares.

Mega-Fudge Brownies

Fudge! Fudge! Call the judge! These are so rich they must be illegal.

1 CUP SUGAR
¾ CUP BUTTER
¼ CUP WATER
12 OUNCES SEMISWEET CHOCOLATE BITS
1 TEASPOON VANILLA EXTRACT
2 EGGS
1 CUP ALL-PURPOSE FLOUR
½ TEASPOON BAKING POWDER
½ TEASPOON SALT
1 CUP CHOPPED WALNUTS OR PECANS

1. Preheat the oven to 325°F.
2. Butter and flour a 9 × 13-inch baking pan.
3. Place the sugar, butter and water in a heavy saucepan and bring just to a boil; remove from the heat. Add the chocolate bits and stir until smooth; blend in the vanilla. Transfer to a large mixing bowl and beat in the eggs one at a time, beating well after each addition. In a small mixing bowl, blend the flour, baking powder and salt. Add the flour mixture to the chocolate batter, stirring just to combine. Stir in the nuts.
4. Spread the batter evenly in the prepared pan and bake for about 45

minutes, until firm on top and/or a cake tester comes out crumby. Cool and cut into squares.

Chocolate Mousse Brownies

Simpler and easier to make than mousse, these brownies have a soft, rich, delectable center.

3 OUNCES UNSWEETENED CHOCOLATE, DIVIDED
1/4 CUP UNSALTED BUTTER, AT ROOM TEMPERATURE
2/3 CUP ALL-PURPOSE FLOUR
2 TEASPOONS BAKING POWDER
1/4 TEASPOON SALT
1 1/2 CUPS FIRMLY PACKED LIGHT BROWN SUGAR, DIVIDED
1/2 CUP MILK
1 TEASPOON VANILLA EXTRACT
3/4 CUP CHOPPED WALNUTS
1/2 CUP WATER

1. Preheat the oven to 350°F.
2. Butter an 8-inch square baking pan.

3. Melt 2 ounces of the chocolate and 3 tablespoons of the butter in a double boiler over hot water or in a heavy pan over low heat. Cool.
4. Stir together the flour, baking powder, salt and 1 cup of the sugar in a mixing bowl. Beat in the chocolate mixture, then the milk and vanilla. Stir in the walnuts. Spread evenly in the prepared pan.
5. In the double boiler or heavy pan, melt the remaining chocolate and butter with the water. Beat in the remaining sugar and bring the mixture just to a boil. Let cool slightly, then pour evenly over the chocolate batter already in the pan. Bake about 40 minutes, until firm on top and/or a cake tester comes out nearly clean. Cut into squares.

Frostings and Toppings for Brownies

How to make a brownie better! Use these recipes to make a plain brownie more exciting, to dress up a brownie for dessert or simply to gratify greed.

Basic Brownie Frosting

Some people like their lilies gilded. This recipe can go on just about any brownie or blondie you make.

2 OUNCES UNSWEETENED CHOCOLATE
¼ CUP UNSALTED BUTTER
1½ CUPS CONFECTIONERS' SUGAR
1 TEASPOON VANILLA EXTRACT
2 TABLESPOONS LIGHT CREAM

1. Melt the chocolate and butter in a double boiler over hot water or in a heavy pan over low heat.
2. In a large mixing bowl, beat together the sugar, vanilla and cream until smooth. Gradually add the chocolate mixture, blending well. Makes about 1¼ cups frosting, or enough to frost a 9-inch square panful of brownies.

Chocolate Ganache Topping

7 OUNCES SEMISWEET CHOCOLATE
½ CUP HEAVY CREAM

A major-league entry in the fabulous frosting category. This is the topping that makes the Ganache Brownies on page 20 so special.

1. Chop the semisweet chocolate fine.
2. Slowly bring the cream to a full boil in a small saucepan, stirring frequently. Pour it over the chocolate and whisk until the chocolate is melted and the mixture is smooth. Chill briefly until thickened, about 15 minutes.
3. Spread over the brownies and let cool until a glaze forms on top.

Bittersweet Chocolate Glaze

The essence of chocolate. Spread this over a rich, sweet brownie, as we did over the Butterfudge Delights on page 28.

I OUNCE BITTERSWEET CHOCOLATE
I TABLESPOON UNSALTED BUTTER
¼ CUP CHOPPED WALNUTS, PECANS OR ALMONDS, IF DESIRED

Melt the chocolate with the butter in a double boiler over hot water or in a heavy pan over low heat. Cool slightly before spreading over brownies. Sprinkle with chopped nuts, if desired.

Peppermint Frosting

Give a basic brownie the flavor of an after-dinner mint with this frosting. We used it on Grasshopper Brownies on page 67.

3 TABLESPOONS UNSALTED BUTTER, AT
ROOM TEMPERATURE
I CUP CONFECTIONERS' SUGAR
I TABLESPOON HEAVY CREAM
1/2 TEASPOON PEPPERMINT EXTRACT

Combine the softened butter, confectioners' sugar, cream and peppermint extract and beat until smooth. Spread evenly over the brownies while still in the pan. Cool thoroughly.

Brandied Frosting

Add a touch of sophistication to the most modern brownie, or top a brandy-flavored brownie with it as we did on page 71.

1 EGG YOLK
½ CUP SUGAR
2 TABLESPOONS WATER
3 TABLESPOONS COGNAC OR OTHER BRANDY
½ CUP UNSALTED BUTTER, AT ROOM TEMPERATURE

1. In a small mixing bowl, beat the egg yolk until thick and lemon-colored. Beat in the sugar.
2. Combine the water and brandy in a saucepan and bring to a boil. Pour the brandy mixture slowly over the egg yolk in the mixing bowl, beating well to prevent curdling. Return the mixture to the saucepan and bring slowly to a boil, stirring constantly.
3. Beat in the butter a tablespoon at a time until frosting is smooth.

Caramel Frosting

If you love chocolate caramels, you'll love the combination of chocolate brownies and caramel frosting. This is the frosting for the Caramel Brownies on page 86.

1 1/2 CUPS FIRMLY PACKED LIGHT BROWN SUGAR
1/2 CUP HEAVY CREAM
1/4 CUP UNSALTED BUTTER, AT ROOM TEMPERATURE
1/2 TEASPOON VANILLA EXTRACT

1. Cook the brown sugar and cream, stirring, until the sugar dissolves. Continue to cook, bubbling, until a drop of the syrup forms a soft ball when dropped into cold water (234°F. on a candy thermometer).
2. Remove from the heat and add the butter. Let cool slightly, then beat in the butter and the vanilla until the frosting is creamy. Spread immediately on the brownies.

Orange Glaze

Confectioners know that certain flavors enhance the taste of chocolate, and orange is one of them. This is the glaze with which we topped our Apple Raisin Brownies on page 93.

½ CUP CONFECTIONERS' SUGAR
1 TABLESPOON FROZEN ORANGE JUICE CONCENTRATE, THAWED

1. Sift the confectioners' sugar into a bowl and stir in the orange juice until smooth.
2. Spread over the brownies while they are still warm. Cool until the glaze sets before cutting.

Maple Glaze

The same thrill you get from maple-fudge ice cream can be re-created by topping your favorite fudge brownie with this glaze. We used it as the pièce de résistance *on our Maple-Glazed Carrot Brownies, page 97.*

page 97.

½ CUP PURE MAPLE SYRUP
I TABLESPOON CORN SYRUP

1. In a small heavy saucepan combine the maple and corn syrups and bring to a boil over high heat. Swirl the pan by the handle to keep the contents from sticking.
2. Lower the heat and continue cooking and swirling until the syrup is a rich brown caramel color.
3. Remove from the heat and pour slowly over the brownies, tilting the pan to distribute the glaze evenly. Cool until the glaze is set.

Cocoa Frosting

A simple and easy way to make frosting with powdered cocoa.

2 TABLESPOONS UNSWEETENED COCOA
2 CUPS CONFECTIONERS' SUGAR
½ CUP WATER

1. Sift together the cocoa and sugar.
2. Beat in the water until smooth.
3. Pour the mixture into a saucepan and bring to a boil, stirring frequently. Boil about 3 minutes. Cool for a few minutes before frosting brownies.

Note: If you're feeling particularly sinful, try this: dip brownies in the frosting, covering all four sides. Let the excess drip off, then roll them in shredded coconut. Let stand until the frosting is firm.

Mocha Frosting

Coffee is one of the many flavors that enhance the taste of chocolate. Try this icing on a rich, fudgy brownie for greater depth of flavor.

1 ½ CUPS CONFECTIONERS' SUGAR
1 TABLESPOON UNSWEETENED COCOA
1 TABLESPOON UNSALTED BUTTER, AT ROOM TEMPERATURE
1 TEASPOON VANILLA EXTRACT
¼ CUP HOT STRONG BLACK COFFEE

1. In a large mixing bowl, blend the sugar and cocoa and beat in the butter and vanilla.
2. Gradually beat in the coffee until thick and smooth. Spread the icing on brownies.

Hot Fudge Sauce

One of our favorite restaurants, The Turning Point in Piermont, New York, offers a dessert called The Obscene Brownie: a dark, fudgy brownie topped with a scoop of vanilla ice cream and hot fudge sauce. We feel we've earned one after a brisk winter hike along the Hudson River! Top your own Obscene Brownie with some ice cream, and this recipe.

¼ CUP UNSWEETENED COCOA
¾ CUP SUGAR
½ CUP CORN SYRUP
⅓ CUP WATER
2 OUNCES UNSWEETENED CHOCOLATE
2 TABLESPOONS UNSALTED BUTTER
½ CUP EVAPORATED MILK

1. Sift together the cocoa and sugar.
2. In a small heavy saucepan, boil the corn syrup and water for several minutes.
3. Stir the cocoa-sugar mixture into the corn syrup and boil until the sugar is dissolved. Stir in the chocolate and butter until they are melted. Add the milk and return to the boil.
4. Remove from the heat and serve hot.
5. To reheat, place in a microwave oven on high for 1 or 2 minutes or heat in a double boiler over hot water or in a heavy pan over low heat.

White Chocolate Frosting

*Beloved by little girls of
all ages, white chocolate
creates a striking
contrast on top of a dark
chocolate brownie.*

3 OUNCES WHITE CHOCOLATE
1 TEASPOON SALTED BUTTER
½ CUP SOUR CREAM

1. Melt the chocolate and butter in a double boiler over hot water or in a heavy saucepan over low heat. Cool.
2. Blend the sour cream into the chocolate mixture. Chill briefly to achieve a spreadable consistency.

Penuche Frosting

The flavor called penuche has nothing to do with pinochle or peanuts, as I used to think in my childhood. It's the particular combination of brown sugar, confectioners' sugar, and butter that creates this wonderful treat.

½ CUP UNSALTED BUTTER
1 CUP FIRMLY PACKED DARK BROWN SUGAR
¼ CUP MILK
2 CUPS CONFECTIONERS' SUGAR

1. In a heavy saucepan over low heat, melt the butter. Add the brown sugar, bring to a boil and boil, stirring constantly, for 2 or 3 minutes.
2. Add the milk and return to a boil, stirring. Cool.
3. Beat in the confectioners' sugar a half cup at a time. Remove from the heat and cool, stirring occasionally, until a spreadable consistency is achieved.

Custard Sauce

Scrumptious over blondies, fruit-flavored brownies and brownies with nuts. Turns any brownie into a rich dessert elegant enough for company.

4 LARGE EGGS
1/2 CUP SUGAR
1/4 TEASPOON SALT
2 1/2 CUPS MILK
1 1/2 TEASPOONS VANILLA EXTRACT

1. In a large saucepan, beat together the eggs, sugar and salt. Stir in the milk.
2. Cook over low heat, stirring constantly, until mixture thickens and just coats a metal spoon. Remove from heat and stir in the vanilla extract.
3. Cool by setting the saucepan in a bowl of ice or ice-cold water. Cover and chill thoroughly.

Meringue Topping

A novel idea for a glamorous dessert. Makes the plainest brownie a culinary masterpiece.

3 LARGE EGG WHITES
1/4 TEASPOON CREAM OF TARTAR
6 TABLESPOONS SUGAR
1/2 TEASPOON VANILLA EXTRACT

1. Preheat oven to 350°F.
2. In a small mixing bowl, beat the egg whites with the cream of tartar at high speed until foamy. Add sugar, 1 tablespoon at a time, beating constantly until sugar is dissolved (until it does not feel grainy when mixture is rubbed between your fingers) and the whites are glossy and stand in soft peaks. Beat in the vanilla extract.
3. Remove brownies from baking pan and place them, still hot and uncut, on a baking sheet. Spread the meringue over the uncut brownies, starting with small amounts around the sides and continuing until entire surface is covered, spreading it evenly in attractive swirls. Bake until peaks are lightly browned, about 12 to 15 minutes. Cool at room temperature.

How to Build
a Brownie House

Here's a constructive idea for those who feel that brownies are the building blocks of good eating. Try building this at the holidays, for a special birthday party or as a rainy-day project to keep little hands busy.

Building a Brownie House

You can vary the size and layout of this house to coincide with the number of brownie "bricks" you feel like baking or to imitate the contours of a favorite dollhouse.

Materials:

7 BATCHES OF THE ULTIMATE BROWNIE (PAGE 18), FOUR BATCHES CUT INTO
SIXTEEN 2-INCH SQUARES (YOU'LL HAVE SOME SCRAPS LEFT OVER FOR THE
CONSTRUCTION WORKERS TO NIBBLE)
1 BATCH BASIC BROWNIE FROSTING (PAGE 122)
1 CUP BUTTERCREAM FROSTING (SEE NOTE)
1 8-OUNCE CHOCOLATE BAR WITHOUT NUTS
1 SMALL BAG THIN PRETZEL STICKS
1 SMALL BAG M&M-TYPE CHOCOLATE CANDIES
1 BOX ANIMAL CRACKERS OR 1 PACKAGE GUMMI BEARS
MULTICOLORED SPRINKLES

1. Use a large platter or tray measuring at least 10 by 10 inches. Using a knife or a pastry tube, outline an 8-inch square with Brownie Frosting.
2. Lay a row of the 2-inch brownie bricks on edge on top of the frosting around the square, leaving a 2-inch opening (one brown-

ie's width) on one side to form the door. Adjacent brownie bricks should just touch each other. (You'll use 15 brownies in all.)

3. Spread the upper edges of the "wall" with more Brownie Frosting, then lay a second row of bricks, again leaving an opening for the door and also leaving a 2-inch (one brownie's width) opening on each of the other three sides of the house to form windows. You'll use 12 brownies for this row.

4. Spread more Brownie Frosting on top of the wall. Repeat the last row, using another 12 brownies. Line the windows and door with the pretzel sticks, poking their ends into the brownies. Lay pretzel sticks across the tops of the windows and door.

5. Spread Brownie Frosting on top of the wall. Lay a row of brownies all around the wall, topping the door and windows. You'll use 16 brownies for this row. Let the structure stand 15 minutes for the frosting to harden.

6. Cut the fifth batch of brownies in quarters diagonally to form four triangles. Spread Brownie Frosting on the two side walls of the house and secure one of these triangles on top of each wall. Let stand for frosting to set; make sure the triangles stay erect as the frosting hardens.

7. Cut two rectangles, 8 × 5½ inches each, from the two remaining batches of brownies. Spread Brownie Frosting on the front and back walls of the house and on top of the two triangles set on the side walls in step 6. Make a roof of the two 8 × 5½-inch rectangles, leaning them against each other supported by the triangles on either end. Use Brownie Frosting to glue them together at the

top. If the rectangles seem soft, you may wish to support them with cardboard cutouts of the same size, set underneath each rectangle. Let the completed house stand 30 minutes for the frosting to harden.

8. Using a pastry tube, pipe Buttercream Frosting all around the roof, doors and windows (if desired). You may wish to create walkways and a garden with the Buttercream Frosting, as well.

9. Break the chocolate bar into sections. Make four of them into a chimney, gluing it together and in place with Brownie Frosting. Use more chocolate-bar sections to make shutters for the windows.

10. Spread Brownie Frosting thinly on the roof and set the M&M or other chocolate pieces in place like roof tiles. Scatter multicolored sprinkles over them.

11. If desired, add green food coloring to a small amount of the Buttercream Frosting and spread it on the platter around the house to form a lawn. Stand up the animal crackers on the lawn.

12. Use your imagination to add more decorations. Red-heart candies will make charming decorations around the doors and windows. Form a row of silver candy beads around the roof in the Buttercream Frosting trim. Stand a gingerbread man and a gingerbread lady in the front door. In the "yard," install a fish pond of blue paper with a border of Buttercream Frosting, and populate it with goldfish crackers. Put Mozart *Kugein* (candies wrapped in foil with

Note: For Buttercream Frosting, use your favorite recipe or the following.

portraits of Mozart and his wife, Constanze) in the windows, held in place with toothpicks. Pave a sidewalk with graham crackers. Turn the kids loose with some basic ingredients and let them build a masterpiece!

Buttercream Frosting

1 EGG YOLK
½ CUP SUGAR
¼ CUP WATER
½ CUP UNSALTED BUTTER, AT ROOM TEMPERATURE
½ TEASPOON VANILLA EXTRACT

1. In a mixing bowl, beat the egg yolk until thick and lemon-colored.
2. In a saucepan, combine the sugar and water and bring to a boil. Pour the sugar mixture slowly over the egg yolk in the mixing bowl, beating well to prevent curdling. Return the mixture to the saucepan and bring slowly to a boil, stirring constantly.
3. Beat in the butter a tablespoon at a time until frosting is smooth. Stir in the vanilla extract.

Liquid and Dry Measure Equivalencies

Customary	Metric
¼ teaspoon	1.25 milliliters
½ teaspoon	2.5 milliliters
I teaspoon	5 milliliters
I tablespoon	15 milliliters
I fluid ounce	30 milliliters
¼ cup	60 milliliters
⅓ cup	80 milliliters
½ cup	.120 milliliters
I cup	240 milliliters
I pint (2 cups)	480 milliliters
I quart (4 cups, 32 ounces)	960 milliliters (.96 liters)
I gallon (4 quarts)	3.84 liters
I ounce (by weight)	28 grams
¼ pound (4 ounces)	114 grams
I pound (16 ounces)	454 grams
2.2 pounds	I kilogram (1000 grams)

Oven Temperature Equivalencies

Description	°Fahrenheit	°Celsius
Cool	200	90
Very slow	250	120
Slow	300-325	150-160
Moderately slow	325-350	160-180
Moderate	350-375	180-190
Moderately hot	375-400	190-200
Hot	400-450	200-230
Very hot	450-500	230-260